# "ELISABETH'S MANLY COURAGE":
## TESTIMONIALS AND SONGS OF MARTYRED ANABAPTIST WOMEN IN THE LOW COUNTRIES

Hermina Joldersma and Louis Grijp,
Editors and Translators

PRESS

**2001**

Reformation Texts with Translation
Kenneth Hagen, General Editor

Women of the Reformation Series, volume 3
Merry Wiesner-Hanks, Editor

Front cover: Sean Donnelly, from 17th century engraving
Music notations: Willem Mook

**Library of Congress Cataloging-in-Publication Data**

Elisabeth's manly courage : testimonials and songs of martyred Anabaptist women in the Low Countries / Hermina Joldersma and Louis Grijp, editors and translators.
  p. cm. — (Women of the Reformation v. 3)
Includes bibliographical references and index.
  ISBN 0-87462-705-2 (pbk. : alk. paper)
  1. Anabaptist women—Religious life—Netherlands—History—16th century—Sources. 2. Christian women martyrs—Netherlands—History—16th century—History—Sources. 3. Anabaptist women—Religious life—Flanders—History—16th century—Sources. 4. Christian women martyrs—Flanders—History—16th century—History—Sources. I. Joldersma, Hermina, 1953- II. Grijp, Louis Peter. III. Reformation texts with translation (1350-1650). Women of the Reformation v. 3.
  BX4933.N5 E55 2001
  272'.8'08209492—dc21
                                                    2001003617

All rights reserved.
No part of this publication may be reproduced,
stored in a retrieval system, or transmitted in any form or by any means,
electronic, mechanical, photocopying, recording or otherwise,
without prior permission of the publisher, except for quotation of brief passages
in scholarly books, articles, and reviews.

Member, THE ASSOCIATION OF AMERICAN UNIVERSITY PRESSES
**MARQUETTE UNIVERSITY PRESS**
MILWAUKEE

The Association of Jesuit University Presses
2001

# TABLE OF CONTENTS

Foreword ............................................................................. 5

A Word about the Texts ..................................................... 6

Introduction ........................................................................ 9

Bibliography ...................................................................... 37

Weynken Claes (d. The Hague, 1527)
Confession ................................................................... 40
Martyr Song ................................................................ 50

Anna Jansz (d. Rotterdam, 1539)
"Trumpet Song" .......................................................... 56
Testament to her Son Isaiah (excerpts) ........................ 64
Martyr Song ................................................................ 68

Claesken Gaeledochter (d. Leeuwarden, 1559)
Questionings by the Commissioner and
Inquisitor (excerpts) .................................................... 74
Letters to Friends (excerpts) ........................................ 82
Martyr Song ................................................................ 88

Lijsken Dircks (d. Antwerp, 1552) and Jeronimus Segersz
(d. Antwerp, 1551)
Correspondence (excerpts) .......................................... 94
Martyr Song .............................................................. 104

Elisabeth van Leeuwarden (d. Leeuwarden, 1549)
Court Sentence .......................................................... 112
Martyr Song .............................................................. 114

Mary van Beckom and Ursel van Werdum (d. Delden, 1544)
Martyr Song .............................................................. 122

## Six Women of Antwerp (d. Antwerp, 1559)

Martyr Song.................................................................138
Letter from Maeyken de Corte to a Sister in
the faith...................................................................152

## Martha Baerts (d. Ghent, 1560)

"O God, thou art my helper good".........................................158

## Soetken van den Houte (d. Ghent, 1560)

Testament to her Children David, Betken, Tanneken
(excerpts)................................................................164

## Mayken Boosers (d. Doornik, 1564)

Letter to her Parents....................................................170
Testament to her Children (excerpts)......................................174
Two notes, from and to her Children......................................176
Letter to Friends........................................................178
Martyr Song..............................................................180

## Maeyken Wens (d. Antwerp, 1573)

A reproduction of her letter..............................................186
Note from a Niece or Nephew...............................................188
Letter to her Son Adriaen.................................................188
Last farewell from Mattheus Wens to his wife Maeyken...........190

Index of Names ............................................................193
Index of Places ...........................................................195
Index of Subjects .........................................................197

# FOREWORD

With the development of women's history over the last thirty years, a number of texts by and about women in the early modern period have been discovered, edited, translated, and published. This has deepened our understanding of women's experience in the past and also allowed us to view major historical changes such as the Renaissance and the Reformation in new ways. This volume is a contribution to this growing body of literature.

This book is part of the series *Reformation Texts with Translation (1350-1650)* (RTT) published by Marquette University Press, Andrew Tallon, Director. RTT are brief theological and religious works from the fourteenth through the seventeenth centuries translated into English usually for the first time. Three series within RTT are in production: Women of the Reformation, which I edit and of which this text is the third volume; Biblical Studies, edited by Dr. Franz Posset, which currently includes three volumes; and Theology and Piety, edited by Dr. Ian Levy, which is in the planning stage. Prof. Kenneth Hagen is the General Editor.

All RTT texts feature the original language and English translation on facing pages, allowing readers direct access to primary sources as well as making the texts available in English. Several of the volumes, including this one, also contain reproductions of the original manuscript or printed texts, giving readers the opportunity to see how these texts would have looked to early modern readers. In this volume, the reproductions include musical notations, a very unusual part of Reformation songbooks. Thus *"Elisabeth's manly courage": Testimonials and Songs of Martyred Anabaptist Women in the Low Countries* contains texts that will be of interest to scholars in a wide number of fields: Women's history and literature, the history of Anabaptism and the Radical Reformation, Dutch literature, music history, and the history of popular religion and spirituality. The stories of faith, perseverance, and dignity told in these songs, letters, and documents may be an inspiration to a wider circle of readers as well.

Merry Wiesner-Hanks

# A WORD ABOUT THE TEXTS

A. Sources for the Texts and Music in this Collection:

Texts from *Het Offer des Heeren*, 1570 (pagination: S. Cramer, *Het Offer*, 1904):

    Weynken Claes: Confession and Martyr Song (f. 246v ff., p. 422 ff.)

    Anna Jansz: Testament to her Son Isaiah and Martyr Song (f. 16r ff., p. 70 ff.)

    Mary van Beckom and Ursel van Werdum: Martyr Song (f. 5v ff., p. 509 ff.)

    Elisabeth van Leeuwarden: Martyr Song (f. 28r ff., p. 91 ff.)

    Lijsken Dircks and Jeronimus Segersz: Correspondence and Martyr Song (f. 67v ff., p. 152 ff.)

    Claesken Gaeledochter: Questionings, Letters to Friends, Martyr Song (f. 182r ff., p. 324 ff.)

    Six Women of Antwerp: Martyr Song (f. 38r ff., p. 581 ff.)

    Mayken Boosers: Letters, Testament, Notes, Martyr Song (f. 236v ff., p. 411 ff.)

Texts from other sources:

    Anna Jansz: "Trumpet Song" (*Veelderhande Liedekens / ghemaect wt de Ouden ende Nieuwen Testamente / die voortijdts in Druck zijn wtghegaen / ende zijn in ordeninge vanden A.B.C. byden anderen gheuoecht*. 1569. [Franeker, erfgenamen van J. Hendriksz.], f. 155ff.; Amsterdam DB: OK 65-306.)

    Elisabeth van Leeuwarden: Court Sentence (Rijksarchief Friesland, rpt. Mellink, *Documenta*, 85)

    Six Women of Antwerp: Letter from Maeyken de Corte (van Braght, *Bloedig Toneel*, 250-251)

    Martha Baerts: Song "O God" (pamphlet of 1579, The Hague KB 1713 F 33:4)

    Soetken van den Houte: Testament (pamphlet of 1579, The Hague KB 1713 F 33:4)

Maeyken Wens: Letter and Note (Zaal Mennonitica, University of Amsterdam Library)

We are grateful to the Zaal Mennonitica, University of Amsterdam Library, for permission to reproduce the letter from Maeyken Wens.

Sources for the musical notation:

Souterliedekens: *Souterliedekens*. Antwerp: Symon Cock, 1540

DEPB: *Devoot ende Profitelijck Boecxken*. Antwerp: Symon Cock, 1539

*Hortulus cytharae*. Antwerp: P. Phalesius, 1582

We thank Willem Mook for transcribing handwritten notation into the fine melodies included in this volume. Our special thanks also goes to Joan Skocir for her wonderful work in transforming a manuscript into a book.

B. Transcription of the Netherlandic Texts, and Translations:

For all texts except Maeyken Wens's correspondence the i/j and u/v/w spellings have been normalized; in the texts by Martha Baerts and Soetken van den Houte abbreviations have been expanded. For Maeyken Wens, the transcription is "diplomatic": it seeks to represent the original (rpt. as illustration) as closely as possible in order to give some idea of the characteristics of language written under extreme duress. All translations are faithful to the original while respecting the demands of English, with some effort made to approximate the scriptural style of much sixteenth-century Anabaptist writing.

C. Biblical References:

Maeyken Wens's letter indicates that exact scriptural references (book, chapter, verse), printed in the margins of texts in *Het Offer*, are later editorial additions. They are included here because they became integral to the instructional aspect of martyrological collections, and because it is of interest to compare the biblical text with the emphases placed by Anabaptists in the martyrological context. Our thanks goes

to Marieke de Boer, who checked such biblical marginalia against a number of sixteenth-century Netherlandic Bibles as well as later translations (including the seventeenth-century *Statenbijbel*, the Netherlandic "King James"), and against the King James; she has ascertained that it was not possible to identify conclusively any contemporary Bible as having served as source for the editor of *Het Offer*. A number of factors may be at play in this: the original editor(s) made errors; the marginalia are hard to decipher and mistakes crept in during subsequent reprintings; a copy of the exact Bible used by the editor may no longer be extant (important because chapter/verse divisions were just beginning to be established).

In this volume the biblical marginalia in the Netherlandic texts are true to *Het Offer* of 1570; in the translations they have been corrected where mistakes were obvious. For logistical reasons they have been incorporated into the body of the prose texts, rather than appearing in the margins. Abbreviations in the translations follow *The New Oxford Annotated Bible with the Apocrypha. Expanded Edition. Revised Standard Version.* Ed. H. G. May and B.M. Metzger (New York: Oxford UP, 1977). Also consulted were *The New International Study Bible*, ed. K. Barker (Grand Rapids, MI: Zondervan, 1985) and *The Authorized King James Version* (Philadelphia, PA: National Publishing, 1970).

# INTRODUCTION

## ANABAPTISM IN THE LOW COUNTRIES

To describe the Reformation in the Low Countries, writes historian Johan Decavele, is, much more than elsewhere in Europe, necessarily to describe the persecution of heretics, for in this part of the Habsburg Empire all Protestant beliefs were combated more thoroughly and systematically than in any other.[1] Such persecution was constituted by an often complex interaction between the persecuted beliefs and believers on the one hand, and the various machineries set up by church and state to persecute them on the other. One must therefore keep in mind that the documents available to us, including those contained here, were born in the crucible of that interaction. There is much in the documents from both sides that is partisan and formulaic; at the same time each believer, and to some extent each persecutor, shaped the record individually through the uniqueness of personality and lived experience. This is also and perhaps especially true for women (and we are reminded that none of the official persecutors were women): while their beliefs were common to the group to which they belonged, women's lived lives included aspects unique to their gender.[2]

Though initially all reformist believers within the Low Countries were treated harshly, Anabaptists (in Dutch called *Wederdoopers* [rebaptizers], *Anabaptisten* [Anabaptists], *Mennisten* [Mennonites], or today *Doopsgezinden* ["the baptism minded," no English equivalent]) soon were more severely persecuted.[3] Insistence on adult baptism instead of the existing practice of infant baptism emerged in various parts of Europe almost simultaneously, and Anabaptism became an identifiable stream within the Reformation very early, in the mid-1520s. Efforts have been made to establish precedent and lead-

---

[1] Johan Decavele, *De dageraad van de reformatie in Vlaanderen (1520-1565)*, 2 vols., (Brussels: Paleis der Academiën, 1975), 6.

[2] The coexistence of group similarities with gender differences is Merry Wiesner's central thesis in her still classic essay, "Beyond Women and the Family: Towards a Gender Analysis of the Reformation," *Sixteenth Century Journal* 18 (1987): 311-321.

[3] They were also more harshly treated: in the wave of persecution of Protestants in Antwerp during the 1550s and 1560s, proportionately more Calvinists were banned, more Anabaptists were executed (Marnef, *Antwerp,* 123; cf. Decavele, *Dageraad,* 609-610).

ership by one group over another, but modern historical scholarship generally agrees that the origins of Anabaptism are "polygenetic," with three primary original groups: the Swiss, the South German/Austrians, and the North German/Dutch.[4] The three Anabaptist groups shared an emphasis on *sola scriptura*, the authority of Scripture alone, as well as the principle of salvation by faith through grace, with the Reformation generally. Increasingly unique to them, besides adult baptism, was a rejection of earthly authority and a criticism of social and economic inequality, though the actions inspired by these beliefs ranged from the voluntary sharing of personal property to the establishment of a (short-lived) Kingdom of God on earth in the city of Münster in 1534. Despite these similarities, the groups diverged somewhat in emphases placed on various doctrines and practices, and the considerable differences in political and social contexts resulted in the movement in each region developing in its own peculiar and identifiable way. Even within Anabaptism in the Low Countries there were differences between the Northern Netherlands and Flanders, one of which was the wave of heightened persecution starting in Flanders in 1550.[5]

In the Low Countries, Luther's teachings had found a ready ear, and throughout the 1520s heterogeneous reforming groups formulated and expressed a variety of criticisms; one of them, the rejection of the belief that Christ's body existed in the host, earned these reformers an early identification as "Sacramentarians." Though Anabaptists shared this belief, Dutch Anabaptism is identified as a

---

[4] The literature on the history of Anabaptism is vast: see the 6,113 entries in Hans J. Hillerbrand, *Anabaptist Bibliography 1520-1630* (St. Louis: Center for Reformation Research, 1991). A good, and brief, overview of the movement and its specific emphases in various locales, as well as the differences women might have experienced, is found in A. Snyder and L. Huebert Hecht, *Profiles of Anabaptist Women. Sixteenth-Century Reforming Pioneers* (Waterloo: Wilfred Laurier UP, 1996). For the Netherlands, C. Krahn's *Dutch Anabaptism: Origin, Spread, Life and Thought, 1450-1600* (The Hague: Nijhoff, 1968) is a standard English-language work; for those who read Dutch, Johan Decavele's *Dageraad* provides an excellent and detailed overview of the Reformation in Flanders generally, and Anabaptism within it; fascinating reading is his clear discussion of the convoluted and complex workings of the machinery of repression (6-48).

[5] Attention to difference between Flemish and North Netherlandic Anabaptists is the focus of A.L.E. Verheyden, *Anabaptism in Flanders, 1530-1650. A Century of Struggle*. Studies in Anabaptist and Mennonite History 9 (Scottdale, PA: Herald Press, 1961). It is also the case that even within places like Flanders there were significant local differences in the extent of the repression because local authorities differed in their levels of tolerance towards and resistance to having local power infringed upon by the inquisitorial process (s. Decavele, *Dageraad*).

movement only after the entrance of Melchior Hoffman, who gave it its peculiar stamp in the early 1530s. A furrier from Strasbourg who fled to the North German town of Emden in 1530[6], Hoffman added to the basic tenets of Anabaptism - belief in adult baptism, denial of Christ's presence in the host, the practice of discipline, the "ban," within the community of the covenant - an overriding concern with his own time as "the Last Days," and a strong belief that prophecy, the work of the Holy Spirit, worked in true believers, male and female alike. Hoffman's ideas clearly struck a chord. He is said to have baptized 300 people in Emden; in the Netherlands Melchiorite Anabaptism flourished, particularly in the cities of Amsterdam, Leeuwarden, and Groningen, and the province of North Holland. Though Hoffman disappeared from the scene in 1533, his vision was taken up by the Haarlem baker Jan Matthijs, and a little later by the infamous Jan van Leiden. Their particular brand of Anabaptism reached its zenith in the establishment of "The New Jerusalem of the Last Days" in Münster in February 1534. The Anabaptists held on in their apocalyptic kingdom for sixteen increasingly desperate months, but Münster was retaken in June 1535 and Anabaptist leaders were unmercifully executed. The events in Münster cast a long shadow throughout the sixteenth century, as proof that Anabaptists were not only doctrinally but also socially dangerous.

After Münster, Netherlandic Anabaptists were led by two men with very different views. David Joris continued to emphasize prophecy and the last days, even if he did not believe that it was possible to establish a visible kingdom of God on earth. Menno Simons, in contrast, emphasized the authority of the Bible and the establishment of a "visible church" of the righteous, though not as an earthly Kingdom. Joris disappeared in 1544 and ended his life in Basel under an assumed name as a relatively prosperous merchant. Menno's version of Anabaptism eventually won out (as we see by the name Mennonite today); his insistence on a "visible church" which did not oppose or even resist authority, even when that authority was intent on persecuting heretical beliefs, resulted in the many hundreds of Anabaptist martyrs in the Low Countries.

What were the Anabaptist beliefs? In the sources a number of doctrinal issues resurface time and again, which has led some to speculate that the Inquisition may have used prescribed, possibly preprinted,

---

[6] See C. A. Snyder, "The North German/Dutch Anabaptist Context," in Snyder and Huebert Hecht, *Profiles,* 248-257.

lists of questions in its examination of suspected heretics.[7] One could also seek the similarity in doctrinal issues raised from case to case in the fact that Anabaptists differed from Catholic orthodoxy according to beliefs and actions arrived at and articulated communally; as a result, a number of key heresies were at issue in almost all Anabaptist processes. Since most of these beliefs appear in some form in the documents in this volume, they are summarized here:[8]

1. Only that which is found in Scripture is to be believed.

2. The Catholic church is not Christ's true church, nor is the Pope Christ's representative; rather, the Pope and all Catholic doctrine and practices (including the marriage sacrament) are false and idolatrous.

3. Infant baptism is worthless: only discerning adults are to be baptized; baptism does not bring salvation, but is a sign of obedience and clear conscience; children who die without baptism are still saved.

4. Christ's flesh and blood are not literally present in the sacraments after their consecration: the mass and the sacraments are idolatrous.

5. Christians need not confess mortal sins to a priest in order to have them forgiven, for priests do not have the power to forgive sins in Christ's name.

6. As there is no purgatory, there is no need to release souls from purgatory through good works or other deeds; the souls of the dead are in neither heaven nor hell but are resting until the day of judgement; neither Mary nor the saints are in heaven.

7. There is no need to observe church ordinances in regard to meatless days, fasting, or feast days.

8. Under no circumstances may one swear an oath.

9. Christ did not descend into hell.

10. It is wrong to call on Mary or the saints.

11. Christ did not receive his human nature from Mary (though what it meant that he was born from Mary was variously interpreted).

12. There is only one person in God, namely the Son of God (a stance which may have been more common to Flemish than northern Anabaptists).

For these beliefs, Anabaptists were fiercely persecuted by Catholic and secular authorities, and in the course of the century by other

---

[7] T. Alberda-van der Zijpp, "De inhoud van de Martelaarsspiegel," introduction to van Braght, *Het Bloedig Tooneel*, n.p.

[8] The list follows Decavele, *Dageraad*, vol. 1, 616-619, who provides greater nuance, for example on Christ's human nature and on the question of the Trinity.

reforming movements as well. Women and men alike were captured and martyred; it has been estimated that a third or more of all Anabaptist martyrs were women, with the figure rising to forty percent in certain areas in times of intense persecution, a much higher percentage than in other groups persecuted for their religious beliefs.[9]

The women profiled in this volume reflect the history of Anabaptist persecution in their personal situations, including some of the local variants. When Weynken Claes was martyred in 1527, her heretical views centred on the Sacraments; and if she held divergent beliefs on baptism, they are not articulated in this early inquisition.[10] Weynken Claes also pre-dates Menno Simons in her rejection of "Nicodemism" (so-called after Nicodemus, the Pharisee who came to Jesus by night) and her insistence on visibility: when a woman urges her to "just think what you want, and remain silent about it, then you wouldn't have to die," Weynken replies that she has been commanded to speak and will do so. Anna Jansz, with close ties to David Joris, clearly advocated an apocalyptic vision of Anabaptism, and her work is filled with the imagery of "the Last Days" found in Revelations; that she was baptized by the pro-Münsterite Meynaart van Emden, who led an attempted revolution in Amsterdam in 1535, makes it highly likely that she sympathized with a Kingdom of Heaven on earth.[11] When in 1544 Mary van Beckom protests that she is not being burned as a criminal or a witch, she may well have been reminding all around her that she was not a Münsterite, that Anabaptists engaged in neither criminal activity nor the horrible heresy of witchcraft. A number of Antwerp Anabaptists, such as Lijsken Dircks and her husband, and the "Six Women of Antwerp," were caught up in the wave of sharply increased repression there from the 1550s on. Finally, it is from the hand of a woman, Maeyken Wens, that we have

---

[9] A. Snyder, "Introduction," in Snyder and Huebert Hecht, *Profiles*, 12, 406-415. Marnef makes the point that of 196 Anabaptists persecuted in Antwerp between 1550 and 1566, 57 were women, while of 86 Calvinists persecuted, only 8 were women (*Antwerp*, 78-79).

[10] See C. Augustijn for a distinction between Sacramentarians and Anabaptists: "Sacrementariërs en dopers," *Doopsgezinde Bijdragen* NR 15 (1989), 121-127. Because Weynken Claes' inquisition emphasizes the Sacraments and does not mention baptism, it has been debated whether she is to be considered an Anabaptist or a more general "Protestant" martyr. She is included here because she was incorporated into Anabaptist martyrology from the 1570 edition of *Het Offer* onwards (Cramer, *Het Offer*, 17).

[11] W. Packull, "Anna Jansz of Rotterdam," in Snyder and Huebert Hecht, *Profiles*, 337-338.

the one autograph still extant from that time, a letter she wrote from prison to her son Adriaen.[12]

## WOMEN WITHIN ANABAPTISM

Despite such knowledge, however, the real "story of Anabaptist women in the sixteenth century is just now beginning to be told": so begins a recent collection of essays on thirty-two such women (seven Swiss, ten South German/Austrian, fifteen North German/Dutch) as well as on more general aspects of women in the Anabaptist tradition. For a time, scholarship on the role of women in Anabaptism tended to polar opposites, with contradictory pronouncements such as "The woman in Anabaptism emerges as a fully emancipated person in religious matters and as independent bearer of Christian convictions" and "the sect showed no inclination to grant women a greater role than they customarily had in sixteenth-century society."[13] The current view is that the truth lies somewhere in the middle: while the Anabaptist movement, too, proves Max Weber's classic thesis that the equality granted to women in the early stages of a religious community's formation always diminishes significantly as routinization and regimentation of community relationships set in, in the early stages from which our texts are taken women did experience more freedom of choice and expression than was the social norm.[14] The nature of that freedom differed from location to location: in the Strasbourg congregations of Melchior Hoffman the office of "prophet" was institutionally open to women, and it is possible to identify a number of active female prophets in the Strasbourg area, but for the Low Countries there is no similar evidence for female prophetic leadership. Rather, Menno Simons emphasized "the

---

[12] The letter, housed in the Zaal Mennonitica in the library of the University of Amsterdam, is reproduced in this volume, with a transcription and translation. The edition by S. Cramer is generally but not scrupulously accurate ("Het eigenhandig laatst adieu van Maeyken Wens aan haar kind," *Doopsgezinde Bijdragen* 44 [1904], 115-133). The accompanying note from a niece or nephew has never been transcribed.

[13] The first from Wolfgang Schäufele, the second from Claus-Peter Clasen, both quoted in Snyder, "Introduction," 9.

[14] Snyder, "Introduction," 9-10; he credits an unpublished MA thesis by Linda Huebert Hecht, "Faith and Action: The Role of Women in the Anabaptist Movement of Tirol, 1527-1529" (University of Waterloo, 1990). See also L. Huebert Hecht, "Appendix: Review of the Literature on Women in the Reformation and Radical Reformation," in Snyder and Huebert Hecht, *Profiles,* 406-415, on Weber 413 n. 25.

'biblical submission' of women to their husbands 'in all reasonable things',", an adherence to certain biblical injunctions and the prevailing mores of a relationship between the sexes possibly informed by the excesses at Münster.[15] Despite this injunction, Netherlandic Anabaptist women were far from invisible. Their contribution is woven into the fabric of their time, and if, with a few notable exceptions (Weynken Claes, Anna Jansz, Elisabeth van Leeuwarden), their stories have hardly been told, it is not because there are no stories to tell. Indeed, the work that has been done so far vividly illustrates what is so often the case in "stories about women": there is more material than one first supposes, and sometimes more of the story has been told than is evident at first glance. In most cases, though, much remains to be done: the scholarship is often scattered, historical approaches have not always encouraged the telling of women's stories, and sources sometimes yield surprising information when approached with a perspective seeking women and their stories.

When one first reads the court records and the martyrological collections on which much of our knowledge of Anabaptist martyrdom is based, one is struck by the relatively high proportion of women mentioned in them. In *Het Offer des Heren* (Sacrifices for the Lord) of 1570 from which the majority of our texts have been taken, somewhat more than twenty percent of the attention goes to women, in the *Martyrs' Mirror* of 1685 by Tieleman van Braght it is about thirty percent, a proportion far higher than in the literature of other persecuted groups. As Huebert Hecht points out, however, research "based only on the cases of women who were executed does not tell the whole story; it neither provides evidence about the total number of women involved in Anabaptism in a given area nor does it shed light on the role of those women who were not executed."[16] Both martyrological collections and court records should be approached with some care because they may each present a less than true picture, the one by idealizing, the other by demonizing. In addition, there is such a similarity in the events as well as the language used to describe them that it requires careful reading to tease out individual stories and experiences. Regardless of minor quibbles about numbers and quality of sources, however, it is an accepted fact that many women were among the Anabaptists martyred for their faith; these women

---

[15] Snyder, "North German/Dutch Anabaptist Context," 254: "This may represent a pragmatic stance on Menno's part, taken because of harsh persecution and a fear of upsetting the social order."

[16] Huebert Hecht, "Appendix," 407.

are not only written about in the records, but are often authentically present in texts written by them.

The records reveal that the experience of female and male Anabaptists in the inquisitorial process did contain some important differences, among the many similarities. One difference lies in the fact that women were in principle excluded from the church and state hierarchy which was persecuting them; the other lies in the difference made by a woman's body, both biologically and the way it was viewed socially. Both women and men were aware of these differences, even if they did not protest them or consider them unjust; the awareness of these differences is reflected in more or less subtle ways in almost every account included in this volume.

What difference might it make that women were in principle excluded from church and state hierarchy and from the authority connected to that hierarchy? In the inquisitorial process, both men and women were confronted as individuals by a larger group composed of professionals with more power than they. But each individual woman was confronted not only by a group, but by a group of men: the soldiers who came to arrest her, the guards, the inquisitors, the secular authorities, the executioners. Each individual woman was put in a position of defending herself against a weight of sanctioned authority and theological learning to which she, by virtue of being a woman, was allowed no access. Still, each Anabaptist woman was empowered by the Anabaptist principle of encouraging every believer, female as well as male, to independently search Scriptures and to share their understanding of the truth with others: the records included here make this point several times. The records also indicate that women's learning, especially when it led to leadership, was a particular problem for the (male) authorities: they were more satisfied with their capture of Elisabeth van Leeuwarden because she was a teacher, and therefore dangerous; they told Claesken van Leeuwarden she would suffer more than her husband because she, the literate one, had been the spiritual leader in the conjugal relationship. Lijsken Dircks is told to tend to her sewing (typical women's work) instead of studying Scripture, and that she tells her husband Jeronimus Segersz of this, and he reassures her on this point particularly, suggests that this was still an entirely vulnerable spot.

The difference made by a woman's body, both biologically and the way it was viewed socially, surfaces in the records continually. When the secular authorities go to torture Elisabeth van Leeuwarden, her main concern is not pain, the "two iron screws, one on each shin," but shame: she says, "Oh my Lords, do not shame me, for

never yet has a man touched my naked body!" to which the procurer general answers: "No, Miss Lijsbet, we will not touch you dishonorably."[17] Despite this attempt at assurance, this anecdote and other similar ones teach that the common fact of medieval torture carried with it for women the additional shame of public assault on a body which had hitherto been held pure through strict privacy. Further, there was the fact of pregnancy; numerous are the accounts in which the act of persecution common to all martyrs carried with it for women the additional burden of callous interference with already risky reproductive processes. Many women were pregnant while in prison, like Lijsken Dircks in our collection; they knew that they would be executed as soon as they had borne the child (and Lijsken's imprisonment was almost six months longer than her husband's because she first had to bear the child). In a letter to her husband, Maeyken Wens talks at some length about this highly stressful situation: "Perhaps the midwife could come again to visit me; and if I wasn't expecting, perhaps she could help me through it; for I don't exactly dare to say that I am expecting, sometimes I think yes, but most of the times no. The Lord grant that it doesn't have to be so, and I imagine you won't miss it if it is not so; my hope is greater that it is not so, than that it is. But I will give it over to the Lord, for even if I cry my eyes out about it, it has to remain the way it is; and it would certainly be a wonder if it were so, since I've been waiting for so long."[18]

This passage is quoted here at some length because the English translation of van Braght leaves out precisely this section of Maeyken's letter. The passage intersects one in which she worries about money, the costs her husband might incur in visiting her in prison; the ambiguity she expresses about the visit (clearly she would like him to come, but cost is an issue) becomes far more understandable when we realize that a pregnancy would mean a longer imprisonment until she had borne the child, with her subsequent immediate execution meaning that her husband would have the care of an infant. We know from her other letters that she loved her children dearly; while it is

---

[17] Cramer, *Het Offer*, 94.
[18] "en oft de Vroevrouw weder quame om my te visiteren / en als ik dan niet en droeg / sy my haest door holp / want ik en soude noch niet dorven seggen dat ik droeg / my dunkt al te mets ja / maer meest neen / de Heere geve dat'et niet zijn en moet / want gy sult'et ook wel ontbeeren / indient 't niet en is / mijn hope is noch meer dat het niet en is / dan dat het is / maer ik wil 't den Heere opgeven / want al krete ik mijn oogen daerom uyt / soo moet het blijven soo het is / het soude immers een wonder werk zijn / dat ik nu soude dragen / daer ik soo lange gebeyd hebbe." Van Braght, *Bloedig Tooneel*, 662.

certainly true that many male Anabaptists similarly expressed strong love for their children, it was only women whose bodies bore them under these most difficult circumstances.

## The Texts in this Edition

The importance of the new technology of print to the success of the Protestant reformation is well established. Remarkable in this context is the alacrity with which Protestants generally, but Anabaptists particularly, grasped the significance of exploiting print as one weapon in martyrdom. When Weynken Claes was burned as the first female Protestant martyr on November 20, 1527, a lengthy account of her debate with the Inquisition was published within a year, with a German translation following shortly, clearly dismaying the authorities who in their judgement had stated explicitly that she was to be burned "so that no memory would remain of her."[19] Early individual records were soon woven together in compendia, in a series of martyrological collections that in the Netherlands culminated first in *Het Offer des Heeren* (which went through ten editions from 1562-1599, with the 1570 edition most cited today). In turn, *Het Offer* formed the core of the famous *Martelaers Spiegel* by van Braght (first edition 1660, second and most well-known edition 1685). It was translated into German in the eighteenth century, and as the *Martyrs' Mirror* into English in the nineteenth (both in Pennsylvania, USA); there are numerous editions of both German and English translations.[20]

In addition to these clearly partisan martyrological collections, we have civic records, for heresy was a civic as well as an ecclesiastical offense; authorities kept relatively extensive records of arrests, imprisonment, interrogation, and execution. Many of them are still in

[19] The many surviving records about the arraignment and execution of Weynken Claes were published in Paul Fredericq, *Corpus Documentorum Inquisitionis Haereticae Pravitatis Neerlandicae. V: Tijdvak der Hervorming in de zestiende eeuw. Eerste Vervolg (24 September 1525 - 31 December 1528)*. 'S Gravenhage: Nijhoff, 1902. The Dutch pamphlet has not survived, but we know that in 1528 substantial efforts were made to trace and destroy "printed records" about Weynken (381); the German pamphlet is also reprinted (271-279).

[20] A bibliography of a century of studies on Protestant martyrologies can be found in the introduction to the photographic reprint of Van Braght (n.p.); the most accessible English-language studies on the Anabaptist tradition are G. C. Studer, "A History of the Martyrs' Mirror," *Mennonite Quarterly Review* 22 (1948): 163-179; for *Het Offer* see Brad Gregory, "Prescribing and Describing Martyrdom: Menno's *Troostelijke vermaninge* and *Het Offer des Heren*." *Mennonite Quarterly Review* 71 (1997): 603-613.

the process of being published; they reveal not only more but sometimes surprising information, and it is worthwhile to return to them in the writing of women's stories.

In this volume somewhat more than half of the texts come from the 1570 edition of *Het Offer*; they are one step closer to the originals than the versions included in van Braght's *Martyrs' Mirror*, though van Braght was quite faithful to his source. It is clear that already the first editor of *Het Offer* must have modified the texts to some degree. For example, the language reveals few of the regional differences that would surely have been part of the original speech of the individuals involved; biblical references are an editorial addition, for they do not appear in other contemporary versions of the material; subsequent editions of *Het Offer* modify spelling to some degree. Still, there is good reason to agree with a modern editor that in *Het Offer* "we have exclusively authentic documents before us, prepared for print by extremely conscientious hands."[21] His conclusion is supported by the considerable differences in vocabulary, sentiment, and style among writers. Though a more thorough stylistic study is still waiting to be done, it is readily apparent that Anneken Jansz is consistently apocalyptic, for example, while Weynken Claes is dramatic and Mayken Boosers calm and detached; different writers favour different biblical passages, and correspondents such as Lijsken and Jeronimus use phrases and images particularly characteristic of them.

Supplementing the texts from *Het Offer* are some from other sources. The sketchy narrative in the song about "Six Women of Antwerp" (from *Het Offer*) is fleshed out with a letter by one of the six, Maeyken de Corte, from the *Martyrs' Mirror*. Elisabeth van Leeuwarden was in many respects a model martyr, but included here is a previously untranslated archival document indicating she did recant. Anna Jansz and Martha Baerts each wrote a song published elsewhere, Anna's in a songbook of 1539, Martha's appended to a contemporary published pamphlet of the writing of her mistress Soetken van den Houte. A portion of Soetken's writing from this pamphlet is also included; it is a rare example of the "advice writing" to children more common in England, for example, and certainly unique for the duress under which it was written. A rare note from children to an

---

[21] Cramer, *Het Offer*, 27, as part of his discussion of the question of authenticity; current scholarship is a little more cautious but accepts that the texts are reasonably authentic. Certainly the only surviving letter from that time, written by Maeyken Wens in 1573, does not cite biblical verses (though it does contain biblical language), but otherwise does correspond to other of her letters included in the *Martyrs' Mirror*.

imprisoned mother (Mayken Boosers), included in *Het Offer* of 1563 but not in subsequent editions, is translated here. And, finally, there is the letter from Maeyken Wens, the only extant martyr's letter from that period (see note 12).

One of the reasons for including a variety of texts is to illustrate the need to piece together women's voices in the sixteenth century from many different sources. For if questions can be raised concerning the authenticity of the voices in the records generally, such questions are even more legitimate for "women's voices." Certainly, with the exception of Maeyken Wens's letter, in all such documents the voices have been filtered through an editorial process; this process was almost certainly controlled, or facilitated, by men, whether that be the court's record keeper, *Het Offer's* first editor, or a song's rhetorician author.[22] The problem of the authenticity of voice, including women's voices, is not unique to these texts, of course, and it will not be solved here. Still, it is possible to be somewhat optimistic about discerning historical women in them. For example, though the only account of Mary van Beckom and Ursel van Werdum is a song anonymously authored by a third person, many of the details are plausibly authentic, such as their strong affection for one another, their steadfastness in the face of family opposition, Ursel's willingness to accompany her sister-in-law, and Mary's gentle words to the executioner at the stake. It may be that the author's portrayal of Mary and Ursel as articulate and intelligent, perfectly capable of answering the questions of far more learned opponents, well-versed in Scripture and stout defenders of their faith, is pure fiction; given the tenacity and courage of Anabaptist martyrs generally, however, there is no reason to believe that the author would have chosen these two women as subject if they had not in essence conformed to that ideal. All in all, the sources present real historical women from every walk of life, with real bodies, real families, and real earthly concerns, celebrating them as models for the behaviour of all fellow believers, men and women alike.

---

[22] Because of lack of evidence, it will never be possible to solve satisfactorily the ubiquitous problem of the anonymity of many early modern texts, including for this volume the editor of *Het Offer* and the writer(s) of all but two of the songs. It is theoretically possible that these could have been women; we take the view, however, that literary women were so unusual that they would likely have been named, and that the default position for author, when there is no name, is much more likely male than female. See also H. Joldersma, "Writing Late-Medieval Women and Song into Literary History," *Tijdschrift voor Nederlandse Taal en Letterkunde,* 117 (2001): 5-26. Anabaptist women did write songs, indeed entire songbooks: see Piet Visser, "Soetjen Gerrits of Rotterdam and Vrou Gerrits of Medemblik," in Snyder and Huebert Hecht, *Profiles,* 384-405.

Introduction 21

## The Special Place of Song

Sixteenth-century martyr song is one of the most perplexing genres for modern readers. To modern sensibilities, the songs seem exceedingly tedious; they are lengthy strophic narratives in often uninspired poetic language, and we cannot fathom their appeal. And yet, appeal they did. One of the characteristics of the Reformation generally was its emphasis on singing religious song in the vernacular, and Martin Luther's writings on communal singing as part of the liturgy (1523) as well as his famous hymn "A Mighty Fortress is Our God" were only the beginnings of a virtual explosion of religious song compositions and songbooks.[23] Luther promoted song because he understood well its psychological and didactic function. Often printed with scriptural references in the margins, songs consolidated scriptural knowledge and constituted a catechism of essential doctrine, all the more easily remembered because of the well-known melodies (especially at first borrowed from popular worldly songs) and the strophic form. They also served to meld a group of individuals into a community of believers by the communal act of singing, so that song played and has continued to play a key role in the life of most religious groups. The earliest songs identifiable as Anabaptist date from between 1529 and 1536; the collection *Een Geestelijck Liedt-Boecxken* (A Spiritual Songbook, c. 1576-1582)[24] includes some written by David Joris as well as the popular "I have heard the trumpet sounding" written by Anna Jansz (included in this volume).

Beginning around the middle of the sixteenth century, there is a veritable flood of songbooks, with titles such as *Veelderhande Liedekens* (Many Diverse Songs) or *Veelderhande schriftuerlijcke Liedekens* (Many

---

[23] See Robin A. Leaver, *"Goostly psalmes and spirituall songes": English and Dutch Metrical Psalms from Coverdale to Utenhove, 1535-1566*. (Oxford: Clarendon, 1991), especially his chapter on "Early Beginnings of Hymnody in Dutch." There was an extensive tradition of pre-reformational, pre-print vernacular religious song carried primarily by women's institutions (see H. Joldersma, "Narrative Songs and Identity in Late-Medieval Women's Religious Communities," in M. Joy, ed. *Paul Ricoeur and Narrative. Context and Contestation* [Calgary: University of Calgary Press, 1997], 97-108).

[24] I.B. Horst, *Een Geestelijck Liedt-Boecxken*, facsimile ed. Mennonite Songbooks, Dutch Series I (Amsterdam and Nieuwkoop: n.p., n.d. [1971]); this undated edition of Joris's songbook is the earliest that has survived though likely not the earliest published. For an edition with commentary, see G.D. Hoogewerff, ed. and intro., *Een Gheestelijck Liedt-Boecxken Inholdende veel schoone sinrijcke Christelijcke Liedekens* [...]. deur D.J. Liederen van Groot-Nederland. (Utrecht: Koninklijke Vereeniging, Het Nederlandsche Lied, 1930).

Diverse Scriptural Songs), with hundreds of songs. A popular genre was the "song of admonition" (*vermaanlied*), considered particularly suitable for new or potential members. Songs were used as we might today use letters, to offer consolation in difficult circumstances and to strengthen fellow believers in their convictions. In addition to these songs, directed to fellow believers, there were prayer songs (*gebedsliederen*) directed to God. Particularly numerous were "songs of complaint" (*klaagliederen*) and "songs of bearing one's cross" (*kruisliederen*) reflecting suffering in difficult times. One of the peculiar characteristics of them all, including the martyr songs, is the marginalia which refer to specific scriptural passages. A comparison of these passages with the songs shows to what extent the language in the songs was imbued with biblical language; indeed, some songs consist almost entirely of rhymed biblical passages. Other songs, so called historical songs (*historieliederen*), have as their subject one biblical story. It was no coincidence that such songs with marginalia were called "scriptural" songs, "made from the Old and the New Testament."[25] These scriptural references had a didactic function: through the song form the biblical passages were etched into the minds of the singers. But they also provided incontrovertible evidence of faithfulness to Scripture. This was a delicate point for Anabaptist song, for despite the many references the songs remained the work of human hands, in contrast to the Psalms and other biblical hymns, which were entirely "God's own word." Especially the Calvinists accused the Anabaptists of singing "people's songs," all the more so when Calvinists had developed their own psalter in 1566. Anabaptists, in contrast, gained the reputation of not wanting to sing biblical psalms; however, though they did object to the militant tone of some psalms, they did sing them.

The melodies of Anabaptist songs merit special attention. Specifically, Anabaptists used the *Souterliedekens* of 1540, unique as one of the first complete psalters in a European vernacular language.[26] The poet, an Utrecht nobleman, rhymed the psalms according to

---

[25] For a discussion of Anabaptist song see Piet Visser et al., *Het lied dat nooit verstomde. Vier eeuwen doopsgezinde liedboekjes*. (Den Ilp: 1988); L. Grijp, "A different flavour in a Psalm-minded setting: Mennonite hymns from the sixteenth and seventeenth centuries," in A. Hamilton, S. Voolstra, and P. Visser, eds., *From Martyr to Muppy. A Historical Introduction to the Cultural Assimilation Processes of a Religious Minority in the Netherlands: The Mennonites*. (Amsterdam: Amsterdam University Press, 1994), 110-132.

[26] *De Souterliedekens* of 1540 are available in a facsimile edition, ed. Jan van Biezen and Marie Veldhuyzen (The Netherlands: Frits Knuf, 1984).

(often secular) popular melodies of the time, melodies to which particularly the young knew "foolish, lascivious songs." Through his psalms, the author hoped to wean young people from the depraved texts by providing them with edifying words to the same attractive melodies. Though a similar intent can be found in earlier religious song, the author of this collection enjoyed unprecedented success: the *Souterliedekens* were reprinted numerous times, and the songs were sung by believers of all denominations, including Roman Catholics. When Calvinists created their own psalm book, however, with specially composed and more solemn melodies, the *Souterliedekens* with its secular melodies became more and more the exclusive psalm book of the Anabaptists.

The most unusual feature of the *Souterliedekens* is that it contains musical notation, in fact separate notation for each individual song; in this it contrasts sharply with other collections, sacred as well as secular, and very much so with Anabaptist song collections. Its more than 150 melodies constitute for us a treasure trove of information about the musical dimension of sixteenth-century song generally. Without the *Souterliedekens* we would not be able to reconstruct the melodies for most Anabaptist songs, for typically these songs have only a "melody reference" (reference to a secular tune by the first line of its text). The Anabaptists wrote many new scriptural songs on the melodies of the *Souterliedekens*, that is, on the originally secular melodies used there. This double background is sometimes evident: for example, the song about Elisabeth van Leeuwarden, included in this volume, can be sung "to the tune of the second Psalm or: 'Rose so red in fullest bloom'." Both refer to the same melody: the second psalm in the *Souterliedekens* was indeed sung to the melody of the secular song "Rose so red." Generally speaking, songs were transmitted in the first instance orally, rather than in written form with musical notation. Singers were not musically educated, but ordinary people most likely unable to read music. Because texts but not musical notation were written down, some of the song collections contain references to melodies which have been lost to us. In this volume we have chosen those songs for which the melody could be traced. In addition to those from the *Souterliedekens*, one melody was taken from a Catholic collection, the *Devoot ende Profitelijck Boecxken* (Devout and Profitable Little Book) of 1539, and one from a music book for

the cittern (which does not imply that sixteenth-century Anabaptists sang Catholic songs, or played the cittern!).[27] The martyr songs with their narrative form about concrete historical events occupy a special place in the Anabaptist song repertoire. It is a genre with a rich tradition. Already Luther's early songs included one on the execution of two friars in Brussels (1523), the first example of the long tradition of the Protestant martyr song. The earliest song accounts of Anabaptist martyrdom likely circulated in manuscript form; by 1562 many of them were gathered into *Een Liedtboecxken tracterende van den Offer des Heren* (A Songbook dealing with Sacrifices for the Lord), published first independently, then bound together with the prose *Het Offer* of 1563. The songs were clearly popular, for *Het Offer* of 1570 advertised as an especially attractive feature that its prose texts had been supplemented by songs written about each martyr; these songs were included directly after the relevant prose texts, while the original *Liedtboecxken* continued to be included as attachment. In his foreword the editor stresses that the songs highlight that which is "most important or edifying" in the material and have remained as close as possible to the actual words of the martyrs, even if the dictates of rhyme have necessitated some rearrangement.[28] The foreword "To the Singer" in the *Liedtboecxken* provides a longer justification for singing, citing the many instances in both the Old and New Testament in which the believer is admonished "not only to read, but to sing," with special emphasis on those instances in which singing expressed joy at deliverance.[29] The editor has gathered both prose and songs in one book, he says, so that the user can read or sing according to mood. Singing merits special admonition, however: "But if you sing, so be sure to see to it that this is

---

[27] A substantial and diverse collection of Anabaptist songs has been recorded on the double CD *Genade en Vrede / Grace and Peace, 16$^{th}$ and 17$^{th}$ Century Mennonite Music from the Netherlands*, by the Netherlandic group Camerata Trajectina (Globe GLO 6038, 1995), including selected verses from the song about Elisabeth and the one written by Martha Baerts, translated in this volume.

[28] "Item, noch sal den Leser believen te weten, dat hier op nieu achter een yeghelijcks Belijdingen, Brieven, ofte Testamenten by ghedaen zijn Liedekens, uut de voorgaende materie ghenomen ende uutgesocht, hier ende daer, dat ons dochte het principaelste ofte leerachtichste te zijn, waer in den Text eygentlijck so na (om tgedicht der rijmen wil) alsment opt alderbest heeft weten te becomen onderhouden is" (Cramer, *Het Offer*, 55). A lovely example of an unfortuitous rhyming effort is found in stanza two of the song about Mayken Boosers, where line one ends with "Mayken" (line 3 provides the rhyme word "payken"), line 2 begins with "Boosers": even in the original, this is hardly inspired poetry. In the main, however, the poetry is average for its time, with some occasional beauty.

[29] Cramer, *Het Offer*, 627.

done to the glory of God." Many of the Netherlandic Anabaptist songs were translated and adapted for inclusion in two contemporary German Anabaptist songbooks, *Ein schön gesangbüchlein, darinn begriffen werden* (1570), and *Außbund Etlicher schöner Christlicher Geseng* (1583).[30] Some of these German texts, and certainly the phenomenon of the martyr song, transcended the sixteenth century: for example, they form a considerable body of the songs sung by Hutterite communities in Alberta, Canada, still today.[31] In *Die Lieder der Hutterischen Brüder*, first published in Alberta in 1916, and based on three manuscripts with origins in the sixteenth century, many of the 347 songs tell of the imprisonment, torture, and death of early Hutterite martyrs.

What was, what is, the appeal of the martyr song? Most of the songs were not written by the martyrs themselves, as they are accounts of their deaths; rather, the songs were composed later, to serve as a vehicle for community edification and "the shaping of a martyr tradition that provided subsequent generations with a sense of history and identity."[32] On twentieth-century Hutterites in Canada, one scholar recently commented: "The importance of singing in the lives of the Hutterites, and the significance they still attach to this activity, cannot be overestimated. In addition to providing enjoyment and a means of self-expression, many of the songs provide the drama that the Hutterites do not enjoy in the theatre: the drama of the many spellbinding stories in the Bible, or the songs about their own martyrs and courageous missionaries."[33] While this seems valid, it is not immediately transferable to the sixteenth century which pro-

---

[30] See a thorough analysis of the genre of martyr song by Ursula Lieseberg, *Studien zum Märtyrerlied der Täufer im 16. Jahrhundert*, Europäische Hochschulschriften, Reihe 1, Deutsche Sprache und Literatur Series I, vol. 1233 (Frankfurt a/M: Peter Lang, 1991); for briefer English discussions see U. Liesebert, "The Martyr Songs of the Hutterite Brethren," *Mennonite Quarterly Review* 67 (1993): 323-336, and V. Doerksen, "The Anabaptist Martyr Ballad," *Mennonite Quarterly Review* (1977): 5-21. Lieseberg highlights especially that which is formulaic in the songs (for example, stock *personae dramatis* include the martyr, his/her enemies, the clergy, secular authorities, the executioner, the people). One must remember, though, that these were also very much the real *personae dramatis* for the actual event.
[31] See Helen Martens, "Women in the Hutterite Song Book (*Die Lieder der Hutterischen Brüder*)," in Snyder and Hecht, *Profiles*, 222-243; publishing information p. 239.
[32] Packull, "Anna Jansz," 342; he misunderstands "van Anneken Jansz" as saying she wrote the song. In fact, martyr songs in *Het Offer* use "van" to mean "about" rather than "by."
[33] Martens, "Women in the Hutterite Song Book," 222.

duced these songs. It would seem that for sixteenth-century Anabaptists, life was about as turbulent as it could be, and little vicarious drama was needed. Rather, one can imagine that their songs, through the shaping of narrative, served to organize these turbulent experiences and to imbue them with transcendent meaning. Besides serving as a primary vehicle for teaching biblical doctrine and for witnessing to the world, the songs celebrated the martyred and encouraged other believers in equally difficult positions. The songs modeled what it meant to be a "Sacrifice for the Lord," portraying in some detail what believers could expect in the course of offering their lives for their faith. The central message concerning this sacrifice was clear: as the final (29th!) stanza of the song about Mary van Beckom and Ursel van Werdum says, "Give us strength, too, in our need / Like them, to battle to the death / so that with greatest longing / we may receive the crown with them."

There is considerable evidence for the importance of singing to the martyrs themselves.[34] Anna Jansz was arrested because on the journey from IJsselmonde to Rotterdam she sang a song which earned her the suspicion of fellow travellers who reported her.[35] When Lijsken Dircks was about to be executed "[s]he spoke boldly and valiantly to the people, and sang a beautiful hymn, so that the people were greatly astonished"; further interrogation by two monks did not deter her, for "God be praised, Lijsken was undaunted and of good cheer, and commenced singing a hymn in the presence of the monks." Imprisoned in a room with a window facing out onto the street, her hymn singing ("Behold, what poor sheep we are") created such a commotion that the authorities moved her to a less accessible location.[36] The comfort that hymn singing gave the martyrs themselves, and the testimony such hymns provided the audience, is the theme of a martyr song commemorating "four pious Christians, bold and fearless" executed at Lier in 1550.[37] As Goyvaert, Gielis, Mariken, and Anneken were led to their deaths, they continued their public protest by singing, and singing so loudly that everyone on the market could hear it; the infuriated authorities ordered Goyvaert muzzled

---

[34] Louis Grijp investigates the phenomenon of martyrs dying with song on their lips in "Zingend de dood in," in F. Willaert, ed., *Veelderhande Liedekens. Studies over het Nederlandse lied tot 1600. Symposium Antwerpen 28 februari 1995* (Leuven: Peeters, 1997), 118-148.

[35] Packull, "Anna Jansz," 341.

[36] All of this according to van Braght, *Martyrs' Mirror*, 522.

[37] Cramer, *Het Offer*, 568-577; a longer prose account is in van Braght, *Martyrs' Mirror*, 494-495.

by a bridle, but he continued to sing in his heart. This martyr song makes much of the martyrs's singing, emphasizing how song expressed their thoughts, gave testimony, and lifted their spirits. At the end, it tells how some onlookers mocked but others sympathized with the martyrs, asking "Why do they torment these people so? Their speaking and singing are all from God!"

## The Women in this Collection

> Thus Wendelmoet Claesdaughter is declared to be a stubborn heretic and misbeliever, by the definitive pronouncement of the honorable Lord, Dean of Naeltwijck, as subdelegated by the honorable Lord, Dean of Saint Peter in Louvain, inquisitor general appointed by our Holy Father the Pope in the territories of his Imperial Majesty hither [Ruard Tapper].
> And so the aforementioned Court, having noted that which was confessed before the aforementioned Dean, in the name of and by order of the elected Emperor of the Romans, King of Germany, of Castile, etc., Count of Holland, Zeeland and Friesland, not wanting the aforementioned sentence to remain without reality, declares that the aforementioned Wendelmoet will be led to the scaffold standing on the square here in the Hague, and will be burnt there to ashes, so that no memory will remain of her, declaring all her goods forfeited and confiscated for his Royal Majesty. Decree by the Governors Assendelft, Male, Ysselmonde, Duvenvoirde, Colster, Cobel, Jaspar Zasbout, Pynss, and pronounced on the 20$^{th}$ of November 1527.[38]

In this death sentence, which accords **Weynken Claes (Wendelmoet)**, burned on November 20, 1527, the dubious honor

---

[38] "Alsoe Wendelmoet Claesdochter, bij sententie diffinitive van den eerwaerdighen heere den deken van Naeltwijck, als gesubdelegeert bij den eerwaerdighen heere den deken van Sinte Pieters tot Loeven, inquisiteur generael geordonneert by onsen heyligen vader den Paeus in de landen vander K. Maj$^t$. herwaertsover [Ruard Tapper], verclaert is kettere hartnackich ende heretijcke; Soe ist, dat tvoirs. Hoff, gesien hebbende tgundt dat voer den voirs. deken beleyt is geweest in den name ende van wegen des gekoeren Keijsers vanden Romeynen, coninck van Germanien, van Castillien, etc., grave van Hollant, Zeelant ende Vrieslant, nijet willende dat de voors. sententie blyve illusoir, verclaert dat de voirs. Wendelmoet geleijt sal worden opt scavolt staende uptie plaetse alhier in den Hage, ende aldaer gebrant tot polveren toe, sulcs dat van haer geen memorie meer en zy, verclaerende alle haer goeden verbeurt ende geconfisqueert tegens de K. Maj$^t$. Actum by stadth$^n$, Assendelft, Male, Ysselmonde, Duuénvoirde, Colster, Cobel, Jaspar Zasbout, Pynss. Ende gepronunchieert upten 20$^n$ in Novembri anno xxvii." (Fredericq, *Corpus Documentorum* #649, 272).

of being the first female Protestant martyr in the territories of Holland, features are present that recur throughout this collection. Overwhelming in these official records kept by the persecuting side is the emphasis on official power: this action is both required and sanctioned by civic and religious structures, and no less an authority than the Pope, and with him the Emperor, has passed judgement in each case. Such authority is not diminished in having been delegated; it is striking how often the officials directly involved are titled and named, as are most of the inquisitors and many of the clerics involved. This authority is emphasized in the inequality of naming, for the "mere" individual against whom judgement is pronounced is identified primarily by first name and family name alone. The legitimacy of authority is emphasized also in the fact that those in authority act as a group, while the heretics stand alone before them. For women, there was the added aspect of the authority of gender, for men per definition could hold authority while women could not, and in this account, as in so many, the image of a woman alone before a group of men is striking.

And yet, in this account as in so many, one other feature is equally if not more striking: the stubbornness of the martyrs, the intractability of their adherence to their faith even in the face of all known authority of the time, and the resulting subjective helplessness by those in power over against the objectively powerless. While this judgement is utterly curt (as they generally were), we know from other court records that it followed intensive attempts to cause Weynken to recant during an imprisonment of over half a year, and that the desperate authorities in Monnickendam wrote to the Governor of Holland for advice on her.[39] The martyrological record of her conversations with various learned men in authoritative positions makes fascinating reading; its catechetical style (questions by the inquisitors, answers by Weynken) lends itself particularly to quick repartee, and if the record is accurate, Weynken was endowed with a quick mind and tongue which she did not hesitate to use in the defense of her faith. One can imagine the horror of the monks as she told them that not only was her Christ not present on the crucifix they held before her, the cross itself was "a wooden cross, toss it into the fire

---

[39] The various records make fascinating reading and illustrate how costly persecuting heretics was for the state (though some costs were passed on to the victim as part of the sentencing, or was paid for in part by the goods confiscated from those executed): for those on Weynken Claes see Fredericq, *Corpus Documentorum* #603, 225; #608, 229-230; #611, 231; #614, 236; #615, 236-237; #649-655, 272-285; 381.

and warm yourself with it!" Her answer to the question of the sacramental oil, though stock for Anabaptists, is equally impertinent: "Oil is good on lettuce, or for greasing your shoes."

**Anna Jansz's** apocalyptic and triumphant "Trumpet Song" shows us a different side of Anabaptism, and another aspect of female authorship. The song is a precious unicum, an early expression of pre-Münsterite apocalypticism and one of the few songs of which female authorship is certain. Anna Jansz is one of the better known Anabaptist women; she also wrote an open (published) letter to David Joris in 1538 and a Testament to her son Isaiah (later major of Rotterdam) just before her execution on January 24, 1539; in addition, a song of fourteen stanzas about her martyrdom appears in *Het Offer* of 1570, expanded into twenty-two stanzas translated for the German *Ausbund* collection. How she captured the contemporary (and the modern!) imagination may be seen in Jan Buyskens's seventeenth-century etching of her in van Braght's *Martyrs' Mirror*: it is an emotional depiction of Anna handing her infant son to the baker who will raise him.[40] Contemporary martyrologies immortalized her as a model martyr, but her apocalyptic perspective and her close ties to David Joris have earned her a label by later historians of "unbalanced, nervous, overstrung."[41] The connection to Joris was indeed of mixed blessing: on the one hand, it is through Joris's songbook that "The Trumpet Song" entered the stream of contemporary song, on the other, Joris's indelible ties to the apocalyptic vision and its unfortunate manifestation in Münster led to a general suppression of his songbook, both in the sixteenth century and in later scholarship.[42] It is reported that the baker who was willing to take Isaiah was a poor man, with six children already, and that his wife was less than overjoyed with the new addition. However, Anna had promised a certain amount of money to whomever would care for her son, and though the connection is not made explicitly, the fact that the wife reconciled herself to

---

[40] See English translations of "Anna's Letter to David Joris" and the German hymn (tr. Pamela Klassen) in Packull, "Anna Jansz," 343-348; the etching, not included in the English translation of van Braght, is reproduced in Snyder and Hecht, *Profiles*, xvii.

[41] Packull, "Anna Jansz," 338.

[42] In his bibliographic work on the "Scriptural Songs" Hofman sketches the contours of this reception: only two of the thirty-three songs in Joris's collection were incorporated into the Sacramentarian or Anabaptist tradition. One of these was Anna's "Trumpet Song," which with some modifications was included in many subsequent sixteenth-century songbooks and frequently copied. (Bert Hofman, *Liedekens vol gheestich confoort. Een bijdrage tot de kennis van de zestiende-eeuwse Schriftuurlijke lyriek* [Hilversum: Verloren, 1993], 257, n. 34).

the situation rather quickly and that the baker's economic lot subsequently improved substantially must have been due not only to his goodness but also to the influx of money into his affairs.

Little is known about **Claesken Gaeledochter** (drowned May 14, 1559) other than the image she creates through her own words in her testimony: her disdain for her opponents' lack of knowledge and her irritation at their stupid questions testify to a sharp and ready mind, and her replies are among the tartest of the martyrs included here. In another letter, however, she speaks eloquently of a great personal sorrow; though she, too, uses the theological categories and idioms of the time, the sorrow seems to border on depression all too familiar to many today. Certainly her words let us catch a glimpse of a highly intelligent and emotionally vibrant woman giving no thought to the cost of furthering a cause in which she believed deeply. Archival records indicate that she was sentenced at the same time as her husband Hendrick Euwessz and a better-known brother in the faith, Jacques D'Auchy (Doussy);[43] she refers to both in her writings several times and mentions particularly that Jacques's eloquence should have convinced the Inquisitors.

The correspondence between **Lijsken Dircks** (drowned February 19, 1552) and her husband **Jeronimus Segersz** (burned September 2, 1551) is among the most extensive, and the most moving, between wife and husband in both *Het Offer* and the *Martyrs' Mirror*. While their letters focus on strengthening one another in the faith, for which they use the current theological idiom of the time, their love for one another is clearly expressed by means of that idiom. Reacting against the charge that they were living in adultery because they had not married in the Catholic church, for example, Jeronimus repeatedly addresses his wife with phrases such as "my beloved wife in the Lord" and "my dearly beloved, chosen wife in the Lord," by which he not only allays any doubts she might have about the legitimacy of their union, but also tells her clearly that he loves her. The discussion of a previous disagreement about Jeronimus's association with someone Lijsken thought undesirable shows that even in a submissive role wives had opinions about their husbands' activities, and that these opinions were taken into account. Jeronimus is clearly distressed that Lijsken's pregnancy means a longer imprisonment (as it turned out, almost a half year longer), since she had to bear the child

---

[43] Cramer, *Het Offer*, 324. The extensive testimony of Jacques D'Auchy (which does not mention Claesken), included in van Braght, *Martyrs' Mirror*, 591-611, shows him to be a classically educated man fluent in French, Dutch, and German.

before she could be executed. According to the first person narrative report in the *Martyrs' Mirror*, Lijsken's plight moved many, and so strong was support for her that the authorities drowned her between three and four in the morning so that her execution would not incite further unrest. Even at that hour there were some witnesses, however, and they reported "that she went boldly unto death."[44]

The story of **Elisabeth van Leeuwarden** (also Lijsbeth Dirks, drowned May 27, 1549) is one which did and still does capture the imagination, although a recently published archival document qualifies the historical picture of unwavering faith in the face of great pain and persecution that is presented in the martyrologies.[45] Elisabeth was "van grooten huyse" (from an important family), educated in the school of the convent Tienge by Leer in East Frisia, where she learned to read Latin. In the convent she became increasingly disenchanted with the discrepancy between the life she found there and that of which she read in her Latin New Testament; her striving for a different life led first to suspicion by her fellow nuns, then to a bout of imprisonment on the premises for heretical ideas. This became intolerable, and she devised a plan of escape by exchanging clothes with one of the milkmaids. Eventually, through the help of an Anabaptist network in which she also became instructed in that faith, she returned to Leeuwarden where her work with Menno Simons earned her the slanderous gossip that he was her husband. She is thought to have been the first known Mennonite Deaconess; as has been mentioned, the inquisitors made a great deal of the fact that she was a teacher. The martyrologies describe the torture of Elisabeth in some detail, all the better to highlight her "manly courage"; if she did recant, the fact that she was drowned nevertheless suggests that she was considered a dangerous heretic, perhaps because she did teach others. She is still to be appreciated as a woman of independence of thought, action, bravery, and leadership, aspects of a "womanly courage" all the more unusual in light of the narrow range of action open to women in her time.

The execution of **Mary van Beckom** and **Ursel van Werdum** (also Ursel van Delden, both burned November 13, 1544), noblewomen from the eastern regions of the Netherlands, excited the pub-

---

[44] Van Braght, *Martyrs' Mirror*, 521-522.
[45] See Cornelius J. Dyck, "Elisabeth and Hadewijk of Friesland," in Snyder and Huebert Hecht, *Profiles*, 358-364, who relies primarily on the material in van Braght's *Martyrs' Mirror* and provides significant portions of Elisabeth's testimony in English translation. He does not cite the court record from Mellink, *Documenta Anabaptistica Neerlandica*, 85 included in this volume.

lic imagination in both the Netherlandic and German regions from the very first. The lack of archival records has led to the conclusion that the "most credible detail comes from the hymns,"[46] of which there were at least four distinct ones, two in Dutch and two in German (in addition to translations); still, there is more information than has been commonly thought.[47] Noteworthy in the story of these sisters-in-law (Ursel was married to Mary's brother Jan van Beckom) is the love between them: when Mary is arrested and asks Ursel to accompany her, Ursel's only hesitation is to ask her husband for his permission; once received, she gladly goes with Mary and shares her fate. The song provides several fascinating glimpses into the dynamics of extended families in these troubled religious times. Mary's mother had banished her from the family home, presumably because of her beliefs, which may well explain her residency with her brother; Ursel's mother and sisters traveled from distant East Frisia (now Germany) to dissuade her from her path, without the desired result, though the song does not suggest final animosity between Ursel and her mother. It is assumed that Jan van Beckom was not of the Anabaptist persuasion, for there is no record of any inquisitorial attention to him, but he must have tolerated the independence of faith in his wife and his sister. The matter did not end with the death of the two women, however. Goesen van Raesveld, the sheriff who arrested Mary, was a blood relative who stood to gain her property upon her death; the next year he reported to the governor that Ursel's brothers Hicko and Hero had written him threatening letters and even sent twelve armed men to carry out their threats.[48] There is none of this in the song, however, which focuses only on the poignant love of two noblewomen for each other and for their Lord as they died for their faith.

The song about "**Six Women of Antwerp**," martyrs otherwise unnamed in the song, suggests that the desire to remember every martyr individually could not always be met because of the large numbers of those executed, particularly in Antwerp between 1550 and 1566.[49] For their names, the song refers the singer/reader to

[46] John Oyer, "Maria and Ursula van Beckum," in Snyder and Huebert Hecht, *Profiles*, 356, n. 1. We thank Barbara Boock (German Folk Song Archive, Freiburg), for providing a copy of an undated German broadside version printed in Nürnberg by Valentin Newber.

[47] A.F. Mellink, *De wederdopers in de noordelijke Nederlanden* 1531–1544 (Groningen: Wolters, 1954), 414-415 gleans information from two other sources; We also follow his naming of Ursel according to her family birthplace, Werdum.

[48] Mellink, *De Wederdopers*, 415.

[49] Marnef, *Antwerp*, 72-80.

INTRODUCTION 33

another in *Het Offer* in which 72 Antwerp Anabaptists martyred between 1555 and 1560 are named.[50] Archival inquisitorial records reveal that these six women were **Maayken de Cat,** daughter of Joos de Catte, born in Wervik, and **Magdalena Andriesdochter,** born in Maastricht, both drowned on July 29, 1559; **Aechtken, Adriaen Jorisdochter,** born in Zierikzee, likely beheaded on July 29, 1559; **Maeyken Sprincen,** born in Maastricht, and **Margriet van Halle,** widow of Willem Eggertings, both drowned on October 12, 1559; **Maeyken de Corte** of Ghent, reportedly beheaded on October 12, 1559.[51] Why the author chose to highlight these women in a separate song without mentioning their names is not entirely clear; perhaps it permitted a starker contrast between the unimportance of earthly existence and the eternal reward awaiting believers: "Their names are not written here / But have been recorded in the Book of Life / With all those who live according to his laws" (stanza 24). The account does place considerable emphasis on the fact that these six were women (stanza 6), the weaker vessel physically and emotionally, but in the faith "as strong as men," and it would seem that the courage of women served as particular inspiration to the beleaguered. The author also makes a suggestive connection between women, pain, and childbirth in the report that two of the women were tortured (stanza 19): the torturers should have known that pain is part of the birthing process (for both child and mother?), and while the stated implication is that these men should have naturally treated the women more respectfully for that, the unstated implication seems to be that women who had experienced childbirth were used to pain and would not likely succumb under torture. Of these six women, we know somewhat more about two of them. Confiscation records show that **Maeyken de Corte** owned relatively substantial property.[52] In a letter written to her sister (included here) she tells of attempts to use the pressure of family members (two sisters and brothers-in-law) to

[50] The six women are named in stanzas 17 and 18 of "Aenhoort Godt hemelsche Vader," Cramer, *Het Offer,* 563-568.
[51] Cramer, *Het Offer,* 581; see P. Génard, *Antwerpsch Archievenblad/Bulletin des Archives d'Anvers* (Antwerpen: Wed. de Backer, 1864-[1934]), vol. IX, 3-5, 9-10, 15-16 for the records on these women.
[52] Mayken de Corte was one of the three (of 127 listed) Antwerp Anabaptists persecuted between 1550 and 1566 to own property worth more than 100 guilders (Marnef, *Antwerp,* 78; cf. Decavele, *Dageraad,* 529). Both Margriet van Halle and Maeyken Sprincen are listed as having clothes, household goods, beds and other furniture confiscated; together with the property of a woman who had broken out of prison, their property made a profit of "two hundred guilders, 13 ½ 'stuvers'" (Génard, *Antwerpsch Archievenblad* IX, 16-17).

cause her to recant, as well as the bribe of keeping such recanting a secret; one might suppose that her somewhat more well-to-do station may have prompted such extraordinary attempts by the authorities. We also know that **Maayken de Cat's** two sisters Barbele and Medarde were imprisoned for heretical beliefs in 1565 but escaped by night;[53] further, her father Joos, headstrong and tyrannical bailiff in Wervik, was positive towards Anabaptists (for example he rented his houses out to them without compunction) and was arraigned before the Inquisition several times but did not lose his life.[54]

The song of **Martha Baerts** (beheaded November 20, 1560) is the second of which we are certain of a female author. If Anna Jansz's "Trumpet Song" was fittingly apocalyptic for the 1530s in which she wrote it, Martha's is fittingly simple for a song composed by a maid in different circumstances thirty years later. We know that Martha served in the household of an Anabaptist woman, **Soetken van den Houte**, who was martyred at the same time. According to the last stanza of her song, Martha, twenty-one at the time, gave herself up to the authorities rather than be apprehended by them; though the historical record does not mention this, it is in keeping with what can be seen as "the power of the powerless" and the way in which the nominally powerless, even housemaids, could take charge of processes and stymie authority. The story of the imprisonment and interrogation of **Soetken van den Houte**, **Martha Baerts**, Lijnken Claeys and Lijnken Pieters bears repeating, for it illustrates this basic principle of power.[55] The historical record indicates that the issues addressed by the inquisitors were the standard ones raised with Anabaptists, and the women's responses were typical: they maintained "that the Catholic Church is not the true Christian Church but the whore of Babylon, that the pope is an Antichrist, that the baptism of infants is without value, and that children who die without baptism are saved ... [T]hey also denied transubstantiation, repudiated the invocation of Mary and the other saints, rejected the existence of purgatory, and expressed their opposition to the swearing of oaths."[56] The "tireless Flemish inquisitor, Pieter Titelmans"[57] was not satisfied

---

[53] Génard, *Antwerpsch Archievenblad* IX, 292-293.
[54] Decavele, *Dageraad,* 489-491.
[55] See Brad Gregory's excellent article on these women: "Soetken van den Houte of Oudenaarde," in Snyder and Huebert Hecht, *Profiles,* 365-377.
[56] Gregory, "Soetken," 368.
[57] These are Gregory's words ("Soetken," 365); for a fascinating and detailed account of Pieter Titelmans, see Decavele, *Dageraad,* 14-31. That a maid like Martha was able to stand firm in her faith despite his onslaught says a great deal about her fortitude.

with this end to the affair, and made at least three separate attempts to convince the women to recant; finally, however, he had to concede defeat, pronouncing them excommunicated and handing them over to the secular authorities. These, too, did all they could to convince the women of the errors of their ways, sending appeals "to the Dominicans, Augustinians, Carmelites and Franciscans in Ghent, asking each to send representatives from their respective houses to try to persuade these women to recant"[58] so that the death sentence could be commuted; no doubt these are some of "the tempters" Martha mentions as seeking to deafen her (stanza 6). When after more than a month of trying, the religious orders, too, were unsuccessful, as was "a team of city officials and a parish pastor" sent by the magistrates on September 7, the women were left in prison for ten more weeks before the civic authorities finally conceded defeat (!), carrying out the required death sentence for three of the women on November 20, 1560. When one imagines an unmarried, twenty-one year old maidservant imprisoned, condemned to death, and beset for months by the most sophisticated theological learning of the day, the stylistically simple song becomes its own "trumpet song," a moving account of simple faith that remained unwavering in the face of even the most troubled times.

The texts from the hand of **Mayken Boosers** of Doornik (burned September 18, 1564) are, according to the later editor of *Het Offer*, "among the finest in the collection: the intimate, warm tone towards her children ... the peace she experiences in the face of death and the manner in which she comforts her parents about this ... all is equally appealing."[59] Daughter of the Kortrijk sheriff Alaert de Boosere, her entire family was sympathetic to Anabaptist leanings, for her brother Hanskin was arraigned in 1553 (though never executed), her father tolerated his children's visits to his house, and her mother sympathized openly with her daughter.[60] Mayken was baptized in 1552 or 1554, but in 1558 fled with her husband to Doornik, where she became a leading figure in the small group of Anabaptists. Perhaps it was, again, particularly her leadership which encouraged harsh action by the authorities; it would be worth exploring further whether women who were acknowledged teachers or leaders were treated differently than either male leaders or women who were not. Mayken's letters reveal a deep love for her family, especially her children and

---

[58] Gregory, "Soetken," 368.
[59] Cramer, *Het Offer*, 411.
[60] The most detailed information is in Decavele, *Dageraad*, 479-481.

her parents, but are clear articulations of her faith at the same time. Mayken's children were dear to her, and she to them, as the note from the children, written in the stiff style typical of inexperienced correspondents, demonstrates; they and their descendants kept a dried-up pear reportedly given by Mayken to one of her children on the way to the stake, a relic still in the Mennonite archive in Amsterdam today.[61]

Finally, the most important "relic" of that time is the only extant letter, from **Maeyken Wens** (burned October 6, 1573) to her son Adriaen (see note 12). Maeyken's death was additionally horrific because of the severe torture she endured, including having her tongue screwed shut so she could not testify at the stake. Her son Adriaen seems to have loved her particularly: it is he to whom the letter included here was written, as were others. The *Martyrs' Mirror* reports that he took his youngest brother (three at the time) to witness her death from afar; Jan Luyken's seventeenth-century etching depicts him searching through the ashes for the screw, which he kept and passed on to his descendants.[62] Records indicate that Maeyken and her husband long held to their faith in full knowledge of the consequences, for they are named as Anabaptists already in a proclamation of January 16, 1565.[63] We learn from Maeyken's letter to her husband (note 18) that she worried about being pregnant; she thought it unlikely, given how long it had been since the last child (three years!), indicating once again how constant pregnancy was a factor for many women.

One cannot help but be moved, and impressed, by the voices and the experiences of the women presented here. Despite the many similarities in their situations, they gain profiles as articulate and courageous individuals who show not only "manly courage" but the kind of personal courage which is rooted in a self-assurance uncommon for women, one which is based on taking personal responsibility for the most important matter in their lives, their own salvation. One cannot underestimate the effect of women being given, and of women taking on, this personal responsibility, nor of the martyrological accounts in which they are heroines for the exercising of that uncommon personal responsibility. Though societal restrictions remained, women not only rose to the challenge presented to them but transformed that challenge into an opportunity for independent choice, self-expression, and action.

---

[61] S. Cramer, "Martelaarszaken," *Doopsgezinde Bijdragen* 42 (1902), 168-170.

[62] Cramer, "Eigenhandig laatst adieu;" cf. van Braght, *Martyrs' Mirror*, 979-983, etching 980.

[63] Génard, *Antwerpsch Archievenblad* IX, 291, also 294-295.

## Selected Bibliography

Braght, Tieleman J. van. *Het Bloedig Tooneel, of Martelaers Spiegel der Doops-gesinde of Weereloose Christenen.* [Amsterdam, 1685]. Photographic reprint: Dieren: De Bataafsche Leeuw, 1984. Introductions: S.L. Verheus, "Bij de herdruk van de Martelaarsspiegel van T.J. Van Braght (n.p.)"; T. Alberda-van der Zijpp, "De inhoud van de Martelaarsspiegel" (n.p.).

Braght, Tieleman J. van. *The Bloody Theater or Martyrs' Mirror of the Defenseless Christians.* Tr. Joseph F. Sohm [1660 edition]. 9$^{th}$ ed. Scottdale, PA: Herald Press, 1972.

Cramer, Samuel. *Een Lietboecxken, tracterende van den Offer des Heeren, naar de uitgaaf van 1570.* S. Cramer and F. Pijper, *Bibliotheca Reformatoria Neerlandica. Geschriften uit den tijd der Hervorming in de Nederlanden.* Vol. 2. 'S-Gravenhage: Nijhoff, 1904.

Decavele, Johan. *De dageraad van de reformatie in Vlaanderen (1520-1565).* 2 vols. Brussels: Paleis der Academiën, 1975.

Dyck, Cornelius J. "Elisabeth and Hadewijk of Friesland." In: A. Snyder and L. Huebert Hecht, *Profiles of Anabaptist Women. Sixteenth-Century Reforming Pioneers.* Studies in Women and Religion 3. Waterloo, ON: Wilfred Laurier UP, 1996, pp. 359-364.

Fredericq, Paul. *Corpus Documentorum Inquisitionis Haereticae Pravitatis Neerlandicae. V: Tijdvak der Hervorming in de zestiende eeuw. Eerste Vervolg (24 September 1525 - 31 December 1528).* 'S Gravenhage: Nijhoff, 1902.

Gregory, Brad. "Prescribing and Describing Martyrdom: Menno's *Troestelijke vermaninge* and *Het Offer des Heren.*" *Mennonite Quarterly Review* 71 (1997): 603-613.

Gregory, Brad. *Salvation at Stake: Christian Martyrdom in Early Modern Europe.* Harvard: Historical Studies 134. Cambridge: Harvard University Press, 1999.

Gregory, Brad. "Soetken van den Houte of Oudenaarde." In: A. Snyder and L. Huebert Hecht. *Profiles of Anabaptist Women. Sixteenth-Century Reforming Pioneers.* Studies in Women and Religion 3. Waterloo, ON: Wilfred Laurier UP, 1996, pp. 365-377.

Hamilton, A., S. Voolstra, and P. Visser, eds., *From Martyr to Muppy. A Historical Introduction to the Cultural Assimilation Processes of a*

*Religious Minority in the Netherlands: The Mennonites.* Amsterdam: Amsterdam UP, 1994.

Huebert Hecht, Linda. "Appendix: Review of the Literature on Women in the Reformation and the Radical Reformation." In: A. Snyder and L. Huebert Hecht. *Profiles of Anabaptist Women. Sixteenth-Century Reforming Pioneers.* Studies in Women and Religion 3. Waterloo, ON: Wilfred Laurier UP, 1996, pp. 406-415.

Marnef, Guido. *Antwerp in the Age of the Reformation.* Tr. J.C. Grayson. Baltimore: Johns Hopkins UP, 1996.

Oyer, John. "Maria and Ursula van Beckum." In: A. Snyder and L. Huebert Hecht. *Profiles of Anabaptist Women. Sixteenth-Century Reforming Pioneers.* Studies in Women and Religion 3. Waterloo, ON: Wilfred Laurier UP, 1996, pp. 352-358.

Packull, Werner. "Anna Jansz of Rotterdam." In: A. Snyder and L. Huebert Hecht. *Profiles of Anabaptist Women. Sixteenth-Century Reforming Pioneers.* Studies in Women and Religion 3. Waterloo, ON: Wilfred Laurier UP, 1996, pp. 336-351.

Snyder, Arnold C. and Linda A. Huebert Hecht. *Profiles of Anabaptist Women. Sixteenth-Century Reforming Pioneers.* Studies in Women and Religion 3. Waterloo, ON: Wilfred Laurier UP, 1996.

Snyder, Arnold C. "The North German/Dutch Anabaptist Context." In: A. Snyder and L. Huebert Hecht. *Profiles of Anabaptist Women. Sixteenth-Century Reforming Pioneers.* Studies in Women and Religion 3. Waterloo, ON: Wilfred Laurier UP, 1996, pp. 247-257.

Wiesner, Merry E. "Beyond Women and the Family: Towards a Gender Analysis of the Reformation." *Sixteenth Century Journal* 18 (1987): 311-321.

# TESTIMONIALS and SONGS

# WEYNKEN CLAES

*Een Belijdinge van een vrouwe, genaemt Weynken Claes Dochter van Monicken dam, Weduwe zijnde, de welcke in den Hage gedoot ende verbrandt is. Int Jaer. 1527.*

Op den 15. dach Novembris, so is Weynken Claes Dochter in den Hage gevangen ghebrocht, vant tslot te Woerden, ende de Graef van Hoochstraten, Stadthouder in Hollant is daer gecomen den 17. Dach des selven maents. Op den 18. Dach is de voor genoemde Weynken voor den Stadthouder ende vollen Raet van Hollant ghestelt.

Daer vraechde haer een: Vrou hebt ghy u wel beslapen ende bedacht op de dingen die u mijn heeren voorgeleyt hebben?

Ant. Wat ic gesproken heb, daer blijf ic vast by.

Vrag. Ist dat ghy niet anders en spreect, ende u van die dwalinge keert, so salmen u eenen onlijdelijcken doot aendoen.

Antw. Is u dat gewelt [Joan.19.b.11.] van boven gegeven, so ben ic bereyt te lijden.

Vra. Vreest ghy dan den doot niet, die ghy niet gesmaect en hebt?

Ant. Dat is waer, maer ic en sal den doot nemmermeer smaecken, want Christus spreect: [Joan.8.f.51.] So yemant mijn woort hout, die en sal den doot niet smaecken inder eewicheyt. [Luc.16.c.23.] De rijcke man smaect den doot ende sal hem eewich smaken.

Vrag. Wat hout ghy vant Sacrament?

Antw. Ick houde u Sacrament voor broot ende meel, waer ghy lieden dat voor eenen Godt hout, soo segge ick dattet uwen duyvel is.

Vra. Wat hout ghy van de heyligen?

Ant. Ick en ken geen ander [Joan. 2.a.1.] middelaer dan Christum.

Vra. Ghy moet sterven, ist dat ghi hier by blijft.

Ant. [Gal.2.c.20.] Ic ben al gestorven.

Vra. Bent ghy ghestorven, hoe cont ghy dan spreecken?

# WEYNKEN CLAES
## (burned November 20, 1527, in The Hague)

*The Testimony of a Woman named Weynken, daughter of Claes of Monnickendam, a widow who was put to death and burned at the stake in The Hague in the year 1527.*

On the 15th of November Weynken, Claes's daughter, was brought as a prisoner to The Hague from the stronghold in Woerden. Count van Hoochstraten, Governor of Holland, came on the 17th day of the same month. On the 18th the aforementioned Weynken was brought before the Governor and the entire Council of Holland.

One of them asked her: "Woman, have you slept on and considered the matters which these magistrates have laid before you?"

She answered: "I remain true to what I have said."

Q: "If you do not speak differently, and renounce your heresies, they will make you suffer an unbearable death."

A: "If that power [Jn 19:11] has been granted you from above, I am prepared to suffer."

Q: "So you aren't afraid of death, which you have never tasted?"

A: "That's true, but I will never taste that death, for Christ says: [Jn 8:51] 'Whoever keeps my word, he shall never taste death'. [Lk 16:23] The rich man tastes death and will taste it forever."

Q: "What beliefs do you hold concerning the Sacrament?"

A: "I hold your Sacrament to be bread and flour, and if you people believe that to be a God, so I say that it is your devil."

Q: "What beliefs do you hold concerning the saints?"

A: "I know no other [1 Jn 2:1] mediator save Christ."

Q: "You will have to die, if you continue to hold to this."

A: "[Gal 2:20] I have already died."

Q: "If you've already died, how then can you speak?"

Antwoort. De Gheest leeft in my, de Heer [Joa.14.c.20., 17.c.23.] is in my ende ic ben in hem.

Vrage. Wilt ghy een Biechtvader hebben ofte niet?

Antwoort. Ick heb Christum dien biechte ick: Maer dies niet te min, waer ick yemant vertoornt heb, soo wil ick de selfde gheern bidden, dat sy my dat vergeven.

Vra. Wie heeft u dese meyninge geleert, ende hoe coemt ghy daer toe?

Ant. Die Heere die alle menschen tot hem roept: [Joan.10.c.27.] Ooc ben ick een van zijn schapen, daeromme hoore ick zijn stemme.

Vrage. Sijt ghy dan alleen beroepen?

Antwoort. Neen ic, [Mat.11.c.28.] dan de Heere roeptse alle tot hem, die beladen zijn.

Nae veel ander dierghelijcke woorden, is Weynken wederom in den Kercker gevoert: Ende tusschen de twee navolghende daghen, is sy van menigherley persoonen versocht, ende aenghevochten, naemelyck van Monicken ende Papen, ende vrouwen, ende van haer naeste vrienden. Onder ander quam oock een vrouwe tot haer uut simpelheyt, ende beclaechdese op dese wijse: Lieve Moeder, cont ghy niet dencken dat ghy wilt, ende swijghen stil, soo en sout ghy niet sterven.

Doen antwoorde Weynken, segghende: Lieve Suster, het is my bevoolen te spreecken, ende ick ben daer toe beroepen, alsoo dat icket niet swijghen en mach.

Vraghe. Soo sorghe ick dat sy u dooden sullen.

Antwoort. Oft sy my morghen verbranden, ofte in eenen Sack steecken, dat ghelt my al even veel: [Mat.6.b.10.] soo het de Heere voorsien heeft, also moetet geschien, ende niet anders, ick wil by den Heere blijven.

Vrag. Hebt ghy niet anders ghedaen, soo hope ick dat ghy niet sterven en sult.

Antwoort: Aen my en is niet gheleghen, maer als ick vanden Sael boven come, soo schrey ick seer, ende het jammert my, dat ick alle die hupsche Mannen sie, dat sy so verblint zijn, ende ick wil den Heere voor haer bidden.

Daer zijn oock twee swarte oft preecker Monicken by haer ghecomen, de eene als een Biechtvader, de ander als een Onderwijser, thoonende

A: "The Spirit lives in me, the Lord [Jn 14:20, 17:23] is in me, and I am in him."

Q: "Do you want to have a Confessor, or not?"

A: "I have Christ to whom I confess; but that notwithstanding, if I have angered anyone, I will gladly ask that person to forgive me for it."

Q: "Who taught you this opinion, and how do you arrive at it?"

A: "The Lord who calls all people to him: [Jn 10:27] I, too, am one of his sheep, and therefore I hear his voice."

Q: "Are you then the only one who is called?"

A: "Certainly not, [Mt 11:28] for the Lord calls all to him who are heavy laden."

After many similar exchanges Weynken was led back to Prison. In the next two days she was tempted and assailed by many different people, especially by Monks and Priests, also by women, and by her closest friends. Amongst others one woman approached her in ignorance and bemoaned her in this fashion: "Dear Mother, couldn't you just think what you wanted, and remain silent about it? then you wouldn't die."

Weynken answered by saying: "Dear Sister, I have been commanded to speak, and I have been called to that, so I may not remain silent about it."

Q: "Then I fear that they'll kill you."

A: "If they were to burn me tomorrow, or drown me in a Sack, that's all the same to me: [Mt 6:10] as the Lord has ordained it, so it must be, and not otherwise; I will remain steadfast in the Lord."

Q: "If this is all you have done, I hope that you will not die."

A: "That isn't up to me; but when I come from the Chambers above, I always weep bitterly, and it sorrows me greatly to see all those fine Men being so blind; I will pray to the Lord for them."

In addition, two black or preaching Monks [*Dominicans*] came to her, the one as Confessor; the other as Teacher; showing her the Cross,

haer dat Cruys, ende sprack: Siet, hier is uwe Heer, uwe God, Sy antwoorde: Dat en is mijn Godt niet, het is een ander Cruys, daer door ick verlost ben, Dat is een houten Godt, werpt hem int vyer, ende wermt u daer by. De ander vraechde haer, den selven morghen als sy sterven soude, oft sy dat Sacrament niet en wilde ontfanghen, hy wout haer gheerne gheven. Sy seyde: Wat God wout ghy my gheven, die verganckelijck is? diemen om een heller oft duyt vercoopt? Ende tot den Paep ofte Monick (die welcke hem verhuechde, dat hy op dien dach Misse gedaen hadde) seyde sy, dat hy Godt op nieu ghecruyst hadde.

Doen seyde hij: My dunct ghy verdoolt zijt.

Weynken antwoorde: Dat en can ick niet beteren, mijn Heer, mijn God, [Apo.4.b.11.] die in eewicheyt eer, lof ende danck sy, heeft my alsoo ghemaeckt.

Vrag. Wat hout ghy vanden heyligen oly?

Ant. Oly is goet op een slaet, oft u schoenen daer mede te smeyren.

Int midden van de Weecke brachtmense te Hove, Ende als sy nu in die Sael quam, ghinck de Monick tot haer, houdende haer dat Cruys voor het aensicht, segghende: Wederroept doch te voren, eer dattet ordeel gegeven wort. Maer Weynken keerde haer vant Cruys, segghende: Ick blijve by mijn Heer, by mijn Godt, [Rom.8.d.38.] noch doodt noch leven en sal my daer van scheyden. Doen sy voor den Rechter stont, luysterde de Monick haer int oore, seggende: Valt op u knyen, ende bidt de Heeren om genade. Sy antwoorde: Swijcht ghy, heb ick u niet geseyt, dat ghy my van mijn Heer niet trecken en sult?

De Deecken van Naeltwijck sub Commissarius ende Inquisiteur las dat oordeel uut eenen Brief op het Latijnsche, ende wederhalende in Duytsch, sprac op het corte, dat si ghevonden was in een mishgeloove vant Sacrament, ende dat sy onbeweghelijck daer by bleef, Ende daeromme besloot hy dat sy een Ketterssse waer, ende overghaf

they said: "See, here is your Lord, your God." She answered: "That is not my God, I have been saved through a different Cross. That is a wooden God, throw it into the fire and warm yourself with it." The other asked her, the very morning that she was to die, if she did not want to receive the Sacraments, for he would gladly administer them to her. She said: "What God would you give me? one which is mortal? one which is sold for a mite or a tuppence?" And to the Priest or Monk (who prided himself on having held Mass that day) she said that he had crucified God anew.

Then he said: "It seems to me that you're lost."

Weynken answered: "That is something I can't improve: my Lord, my God, [Rev 4:11] to whom be honour, praise and thanks for ever, has made me thus."

Q: "What do you believe concerning the holy oil?"

A "Oil is good on a salad, or for greasing your shoes."[1]

In the middle of the Week they brought her to the judicial authorities. And as she came into the Chamber, the Monk went to her, holding the Cross before her face, saying: "Recant beforehand, before the judgement is passed!" But Weynken turned her face from that Cross, saying: "I will remain steadfast in my Lord, in my God, [Rom 8:38] neither death nor life will separate me from him." When she stood before the Judge, the Monk whispered in her ear, saying: "Fall on your knees, and beg the Magistrates for mercy." She answered: "Silence, you, didn't I tell you that you should not draw me away from my Lord?"

The Dean of Naeltwijck, Sub-Commissioner and Inquisitor,[2] read the judgement from a Letter, first in Latin and repeating it in Dutch: he said in very brief words that she had been found to hold heretical beliefs concerning the Sacrament, and that she remained unmovable in this. Therefore he concluded that she was a Heretic, and handed

---

[1] The image of the holy (sacramental) oil as good for salad or greasing boots appears in reformist literature in England, the Netherlands, and Switzerland: s. A. Duke, "The Face of Popular Dissent in the Low Countries," *Journal of Ecclesiastical History* 26 (1975): 52-53.

[2] The Inquisitor-General for this area, the Dean of Louvain, delegated the Dean of Naeltwijck to act on his behalf. For Weynken the Sub-Inquisitor was Pieter van der Goude, the Inquisitor-General was Nicolaas Coppin (J.C. van Slee, "Wendelmoet Claesdochter van Monnikendam 20 November 1527," *Nederlandsch Archief voor Kerkgeschiedenis* 20 [1927], 135).

Weynken inde Weerlijcke handt, met der Protest. dat hy in haren doot niet en verwillichde. Daer nae ginck hy uut den Raedt, met zijn twee Bysitters, als geestelijcke Mannen.

Van stonden aen werdt by den Cancelier ghelesen, als dat sy (nae segghen) halstarrich ware ghevonden, het welcke niet onghestraft en mochte blijven, Ende dat sy tot pulver soude ghebrandt worden, ende haer goederen al gheconfisqueert worden. Doen sprack Weynken: Ist nu al geschiet? Ick bidde u alle, oft ick yemandt misdaen ofte vertorent hadde, dat ghy my dat vergheven wilt. Doen sprack de Monick tot haer: Cusset nu uwen Heere uwen Godt een mael. Sy antwoorde: Dat en is mijn Heer niet. Int afgaen van de Raedtcamer sprack de Monick tot haer, dat si onse lieve Vrou soude aenroepen, dat sy voor haer bidden soude.

Sy antwoorde: Onse Vrou is in Godt wel te vreden.

Monick. Roeptse aen.

Weynken. Wy hebben [Rom.8.d.34.] Christum die sidt ter rechterhandt zijns Vaders, die bidt voor ons.

Als sy nu van de Sael quam, ende ghinck ter Galghen ofte Gherecht, so seyde de Monick: Siet u Heer een mael aen, die voor u ghestorven is.

Weynken. Dat en is mijn Heer mijn Godt niet, mijn Heer Godt [Joa.14.c.20., 17.c.23] is in my, ende ick ben in hem.

Mon. Siet om, wildy alle die schaepkens veroordeelen, ende zijn sy alle verdoemt?

Weynk. Niet al, [Heb.10.d.30.] dat oordeel behoort Godt toe.

Monic. Vreest ghy u voor dat strenghe oordeel Godts niet?

Weynk. [Luc.9.f.56., Joan.3.b.17., 12.e.47.] God en coemt niet de sondaers te oordeelen, dan om vrede te gheven.

Mon. Vreest ghy niet dat oordeel, dat ghy in een vyer sult lijden?

Weynken. Neen ick, want ick weet, hoe ick met mijnen Heer stae.

Op den Gherust oft Schavot stondt daer een by, die sprack tot Weynken, segghende: Moeder, keert u om tot den volcke, ende bidtse, oft ghy iemandt vertoornt hadt, dat zijt u vergheven. Dat deede sy. Daer

Weynken over to the Secular authorities, with the Protest that he did not consent to her death. Then he and his two Associates, as religious Men, left the Council.

Immediately thereupon the following was read out by the Chancellor: as was reported, she had been found intractable, which could not remain unpunished; she was to be burned to ashes, and her property entirely confiscated. Then Weynken spoke: "Is it all over with? I pray you all, if I have injured or angered anyone, that you will forgive me." Then the Monk said to her: "Now kiss the Lord your God just once." She answered: "That is not my Lord." While leaving the Council Room the Monk told her to call on Our Dear Lady, asking her to intercede for her.

She replied: "Our Lady is at peace in God."

Monk: "Call on her!"

Weynken: "We have [Rom 8:34] Christ, who sits at the right hand of his father, he intercedes for us."

As she now left the Chamber, and went to the Scaffold or the Execution, the Monk said: "Look upon your Lord, who has died for you!"

Weynken: "That is not my Lord my God: my Lord God [Jn 14:20, 17:23] is in me, and I am in him."

Monk: "Look around you, would you condemn all these little sheep, and are they all damned?"

Weynken: "Not all of them: [Heb 10:30] judgement belongs to God alone."

Monk: "Do you not fear the severe judgement of God?"

Weynken: "[Lk 9:55, Jn 3:17, 12:47] God does not come to condemn sinners, but to bring them peace."

Monk: "Do you not fear judgement, that you shall suffer in a fire?"

Weynken: "No, not I, for I trust my relationship with God."

On the Platform or Scaffold there was standing an assistant who spoke to Weynken, saying: "Mother, turn yourself to the people, and pray them, that if you have angered anyone, they will forgive you." That

nae holp sy den Meester dat pulver inden boesem steecken. Hier versochtse de Monick wederom met dat Cruys, het welcke sy metter handt van haer stiet, ende keerde haer om, seggende: Hoe tenteerdy my, [Act.7.g.55.] Myn Heer mijn Godt is hier boven. Daer nae ghinck sy vrolijck, als oft sy tot eender Hoochtijt soude ghaen, ende sy en ontsette haer aensicht niet eens voor dat vyer. De Monick seyde: Wildy niet steets ende vast by Godt blijven?

Weynk. Jae ick voorwaer.

Monick. Nu moet ghy terstont int vyer ghaen, nu wederroept noch.

Weynk. Ick ben wel te vreden [Mat.6.b.10.] des Heeren wille moet gheschien.

Monick. Dat en is des Heeren wil niet, de wille Godts is uwe heylighinghe.

De Hencker sprack: Moeder blijft by Godt, ende laet u van Godt niet trecken. Midlertijt ghinck dese vrome Heldin alleen onvervaert nae de banck toe, ende voechde haer selfs aen den Staeck, daer aen mense verbranden soude, ende seyde alsoo: Staet de banck oock vast, sal ick niet vallen? Daer nae heeft die Hencker de coorden bereydt, daermede dat hyse worgen soude, de vrouwe dede af haren halsdoeck oft sluyer, ende voechde de strop aen haren Hals.

Doen riep de Monick: Wendelmoey wilt ghy oock gheern sterven als een Christen mensche?

Antwoort. Jae ick.

Vrage. Ghy verloochent alle Ketterie.

Antwoort. Jae ick.

Vraghe. Dat is ghoet. Daer en boven ist u oock leedt, dat ghy ghedwaelt hebt.

Antw. Ick heb voormaels wel ghedwaelt, dat is my leedt, maer dit en is gheen dwalen, maer den rechten wech, ende ick blijve by Godt.

Als sy nu dat ghesproocken hadde, doen ghinck die Hencker toe, om haer te verworghen, ende als sy dat ghevoelde, sloech sy haer ooghen neder ende hupsch toe, als oft sy in eenen slaep gevallen waer, ende heeft den gheest ghegheven, den twintichsten Dach Novembris. Anno. 1527.

she did. After that she helped the Chief Executioner put the powder[3] into her bosom. Now again the Monk tempted her with the Cross, which she thrust away with her hand; she turned aside, saying: "How are you tempting me? [Acts 7:55] My Lord, my God, is up above." After that she went joyfully, as if she were going to a Wedding Feast, and she did not flinch even when she saw the fire. The Monk said: "Will you not remain steadfastly and firmly with God?"

Weynken: "Surely, I will."

Monk: "In a moment you will have to enter the fire, now do yet recant!"

Weynken: "I am completely content, [Mt 6:10] the Lord's will must come to pass."

Monk: "That is not the Lord's will, the will of God is that you be saved!"

The Executioner said: "Mother, remain with God, do not let yourself be drawn away from God!" Meanwhile this courageous Heroine went up to the stack alone, without fear, even positioning herself by the Stake at which they were going to burn her, and said: "Are you sure the stack is solid, so that I won't fall?" After that the Executioner prepared the ropes with which he was to strangle her. The woman removed her neckerchief or head cloth and put the noose around her neck.

Then the Monk called: "Wendelmoet, wouldn't you like to die as a Christian?"

Weynken: "Yes, indeed I would."

Monk: "So you renounce all Heresy?"

Weynken: "Yes, indeed I do."

Monk: "That is good! Besides that, you are sorry because you have erred."

Weynken: "Previously I did indeed err, and I grieve about that; this is not erring, but the right path, and I remain steadfast in God."

When she had said this, the Executioner began to strangle her; and when she felt that, she lowered her eyes and closed them gently, as if she had fallen asleep, and gave up the ghost, the 20th Day of November 1527.

---

[3] Two common methods of mitigating the extreme pain of death by fire were strangulation and the one mentioned here, a sack of powder on the chest; the powder would be ignited at the same time as the main fire, with the result that the victim would be asphyxiated. Weynken's death seems to have included both, with the strangulation causing the actual death.

*Een Liedeken van Weynken Claes dochter*

Na de wijse: Het was een Joden dochter

*Melody: DEPB, fol.46r*

1  De Heer moet zijn ghepresen
   Van zijn goedertierenheyt
   Dat hy altijt wil wesen
   By die nieu zijn verresen     Rom.6.a.4., Coll.3.a.1.
   En hebben tquaet afgheleyt.

2  Dit machmen claerlijck sporen
   Aen die vrouwe Weynken Claes
   Uut God zijnde gheboren     1.Joan.3.a.9.
   Wiens woort sy had vercoren     Ps.119.l.103.
   Tot haerder troost ende solaes.

3  Gevaen lietmen haer bringen
   In den Haech voor dOverheyt
   Met vragen sy haer aenginghen
   Of sy bleef by die dingen
   Die sy voor heen had gheseyt.

*A Song about Weynken Claes Daughter*
To the Tune: "There was once a Jew's Daughter"

1    The Lord he must be praised
    For all his tender mercies,
    That he will always be
    With those who've risen anew     Rom 6:4, Col 3:1
    And wickedness have cast off.

2    This can be seen most clearly
    In the woman Weynken Claes:
    For she had been born of God,     1 Jn 3:9
    And his word had she chosen     Ps 119:103
    For her comfort and solacement.

3    As prisoner they had her brought
    To The Hague, before the Court;
    With questions they attacked her:
    Did she still affirm those things
    That she in previous times had said?

4   Tgeen dat ick heb gesproocken
    Blijf ick vast by, heeft sy verclaert
    Sy mochten tvyer wel stoocken
    Om branden ende roocken
    Sy was daer niet voor vervaert.

5   Een wasser die daer taelde
    Vraechde noch vant Sacrament
    Daer op Weynken verhaelde
    Dat meel was datmen maelde
    En tbroot eenen Duyvel blent.

6   Hy seyde: Ghy moet sterven
    Ist saeck dat ghy hier by blijft
    Maer om tRijck Gods te erven
    En die Croon te verwerven        2.Ti.4.a.8., Apo.2.b.10.
    Was sy door Gods cracht gestijft.

7   Dus ist oordeel gegeven
    Dat sy sou worden verbrant
    Maer duer Gods geest gedreven
    Gaf sy willich haer leven
    Over in des Heeren hant.

8   Die Monick sachmen loopen
    Om die vrouwe met zijn cruys
    Die lueghenen met hoopen
    Ginck hy aldaer ontknoopen
    Om haer brengen tot confuys.

9   Hy haer also seer quelden
    Dat jammer was en verdriet
    De Buel dies oock ontstelden
    Moeder (was zijn vermelden)
    Laet u van Godt trecken niet.

10  Sy halp den pulver steecken
    Selfs tot haren bosem in
    Siet wat daer is gebleecken
    Van selfs is sy ghestreecken
    Totten pael als een Heldin.

4   "That which I before have spoken,"
    She declared, "I stay steadfast in that."
    They could stoke the fire all they wanted,
    Getting it to burn and smoke:
    She had no fear for any of it.

5   There was one who did the speaking,
    Again asked of the Sacrament;
    To which Weynken did respond,
    'T was flour, naught else, that was milled,
    And the bread a foolish Devil.

6   He said: "Die you must,
    If to this you do hold fast!"
    But to inherit God's own Kingdom
    And the Crown of Life to earn,   2 Tim 4:8, Rev 2:10
    She was strengthened by God's might.

7   And thus was the sentence passed,
    That she was to be burned;
    But by God's spirit driven
    She gave her life most willingly
    Over in the Lord's own hand.

8   The Monk was seen dashing about
    Around that woman with his cross;
    Those lies, a pack of them indeed,
    He was undoing there,
    To bewilder and confuse her.

9   He tormented her to such degree
    That there was sorrow and lamenting;
    This moved even the Deathsman,
    "Mother," (he said to her indeed),
    "Let yourself not be drawn from God!"

10  She herself did help him put
    The powder in her bosom.
    Listen to what happened there:
    Of her own accord she went
    Up to the stake, a Heroine.

11  Sprack: sal ick niet afvallen
    En staet de bancke oock vast
    Daer ginck de Monick rallen
    En had met zijn loos callen
    Die vrouwe noch geern verrast.

12  Mer sy ginc haer selfs voegen
    Seer blijdelijc aen den pael
    Wel ginct na haer genoegen
    Maer die Sophisten wroegen
    En Godloosen altemael.

13  De Buel trat aen om worgen
    Doen sloot sy haer oogen fijn
    Hebbende int hert verborghen
    Een trooster niet om sorgen
    Verlangende thuys te zijn     2.Cor.5.a.8., Phil.1.c.26.

14  Dus lieffelijck ontslapen      Act.7.g.60.
    Is Wendelmoe in den Heer
    Maer Monicken en Papen
    Die naet Christen bloet gapen
    Versaet worden sy nemmermeer.

    FINIS.

11  She spoke: "Won't I fall off?
    And is the stack made fast?"
    Then the monk began to blather,
    And with his deceitful babble,
    Gladly'd have caught her unawares.

12  But she went and placed herself
    So joyfully at the stake;
    Things were going as she wanted.
    But the Sophists kept accusing,[4]
    As did the Godless, all of them.

13  The Deathsman stepped up to strangle -
    Then she closed her eyes so sweet,
    Having in her heart concealed
    A comforter, who took all fear,
    Longing to be home at last.        2 Cor 5:8, Phil 1:23

14  Thus Wendelmoet so sweetly
    In the Lord did fall asleep.       Acts 7:60
    But all those Monks and all Priests, too,
    Whose mouths gape wide for Christian blood,
    Sated and full they'll never be!

---

[4] "Wroegen" is problematic, as it is in the present tense and has no direct object; it does mean to persist in (false) accusations, a common motif in martyrological literature, which is likely its meaning here. Its form may be as it is in order to facilitate rhyme.

# ANNA JANSZ

Na de wijse, Na Oostlandt wil ick varen.

Ick hoo-re de Ba-suy-ne bla-sen, seer ver-re hoor ick tge-schal In Je-ru-sa-lem, in E-dom ba-sen, de bo-den roe-pen o-ver al. Haer ge-luyt gaet in mijn ver-sin-nen: maect u ter Bruy-loft ge-reet, al die den Co-ninck be-min-nen, de Poor-te is o-pen, gaet bin-nen, ver-ciert u, doet aen u Bruy-lofts cleet.

*Melody: Souterliedeken 82*

# ANNA JANSZ
## (drowned January 24, 1539 in Rotterdam)

### *Anna Jansz's "Trumpet Song"*[1]

To the Tune: "To the East Lands will I travel"

1    I hear the Trumpet sounding,
From far off I hear her blast!
In Jerusalem, Edom, in Bashan,
The heralds cry high and low,
To me their sound brings this to mind:
"Prepare yourselves for the wedding feast,
All you who love the King!
The Gate is open, enter in!
Adorn yourselves, don your Wedding finery!"

---

[1] We include the version from *Veelderhande Liedekens* (1569) as one which was republished often in the sixteenth century.

1   Ick hoore de Basuyne blassen,
    seer verre hoor ick tgeschal
    In Jerusalem, in Edom basen,
    de boden roepen over al.
    Haer geluyt gaet in mijn versinnen;
    maect u ter Bruyloft gereet,
    al die den Coninck beminnen,
    de Poorte is open, gaet binnen,
    verciert u, doet aen u Bruylofts cleet.         Mat.22.b.11

2   O Sion, van God uutgelesen,
    hebt ghy haer stemme niet gehoort?
    En wilt doch niet onhoorich wesen,
    maer ontfangt des Heeren Woort.
    Ghy hebt genade vercregen,
    neemt waer het wort u geseyt,
    ras maect u op de wegen,
    eer ghy met Babilon wort versleghen,            Apo.18.b.10
    haest u seere, niet en verbeyt.

3   Dat teecken Thau is u gegeven,                  Ezech.9.a.4
    dat Ezechiel int negenste staet:
    Des Heeren knechten worden bescreven,           Apo.7.a.3
    die volbrengen des Heeren Raet.
    O Sion, besluyt u verclaerden,                  4.Es.2.e.40
    u getal is schier vervult
    van die haer leven niet en swaerden,            Apo.12.b.16
    ghecocht zijnde vander Aerden,                  Apo.6.a.4
    tlam heeft betaelt voor haer de schult.

4   O Thoren Eder vercooren,                       Gen.35.6.21
    o vergulden Roose coemt nu met macht,
    Wilt nu u hooft op booren,
    dat ghy des Heeren toecoemst verwacht.
    Wat wilt ghy een ander aenhangen,
    oft ghy den Coninck niet crijgen en sout?
    dat wee heeft u bevangen,                      Esa.26.b.17
    hierom is u also bange
    als een vrou in baren menichfout.

5   Staet op, Sion, wapent u leden,                Mic.4.b.13
    maect u totten strijde bereet.

| | | |
|---|---|---|
| 1 | I hear the Trumpet sounding, | |
| | From far off I hear her blast! | |
| | In Jerusalem, Edom, in Bashan, | |
| | The heralds cry high and low, | |
| | To me their sound brings this to mind: | |
| | "Prepare yourselves for the wedding feast, | |
| | All you who love the King! | |
| | The Gate is open, enter in! | |
| | Adorn yourselves, don your Wedding finery!" | Mt 22:11 |
| | | |
| 2 | O Zion, God's special chosen, | |
| | Have you not heard her voice? | |
| | Do not disobey willfully, | |
| | But accept the Word of the Lord. | |
| | You have been granted mercy, | |
| | Make good use of it, you're being warned! | |
| | Quick, hurry, get on your way, | |
| | Before you, with Babylon together are slain - | Rev 18:10 |
| | Make haste, make haste, do not delay! | |
| | | |
| 3 | The sign of Thau has been given you, | Ezek 9:4 |
| | The one in Ezekiel, chapter nine: | |
| | The Lord's servants are now being marked, | Rev 7:3 |
| | By those who fulfil the Lord's decree. | |
| | Oh Zion, conclude the list of transfigured! | 2 Es 2:40 |
| | Your number will soon be complete, | |
| | By them whose lives did not weigh heavy, | Rev 12:11(?) |
| | Having been redeemed from the Earth, | Rev 6:9(?) |
| | The lamb has paid their debt for them. | |
| | | |
| 4 | O Tower of Eder, chosen, elected, | Gen 35:21 |
| | O gilded Rose, come now with power! | |
| | Now is the time to lift up your heads, | |
| | So that you expect the coming of the Lord! | |
| | Why would you want to belong to another | |
| | When that would mean you would lose the King? | |
| | The sharpest pain has overwhelmed you, | Is 26:17 |
| | And caused you to be just as fearful | |
| | a woman who in childbirth labors. | |
| | | |
| 5 | Arise, O Zion, gird your loins, | Mic 4:13 |
| | Prepare yourself for battle. | |

|   | Ghy moet den engen wech in treden, | Mat.7.b.13 |
|---|---|---|
|   | maer eens menschen voetstap breet: | |
|   | Den inganck leyt int verneren, | |
|   | daer ghy u erfdeel sult ontfaen, | |
|   | en vreest niet al sidy teere | |
|   | voor den Arent met zijnen veeren, | 4.Esdr.11 |
|   | hy sal u met zijnen clauwen slaen. | |
| 6 | Die Draeck is comen opter Aerde | Apo.12.a.8 |
|   | en is bevangen met grooter nijt, | |
|   | Want die Vrouwe, diet Manneken baerde, | |
|   | is hem ontnomen, dus maect hy strijt, | |
|   | Om tegen haer Saet te vechten: | |
|   | sijt goets moets, en twijfelt niet, | |
|   | onsen Leydtman coemt schier om rechten | |
|   | ordeel houden met zijnen knechten, | Jude.b.14 |
|   | hy salse verlossen uut alle verdriet. | |
| 7 | O wakers op Sions tooren, | Esa.52.a.8, 62.a.6 |
|   | my dunct, dat sweert is nu bereyt: | |
|   | Laet u Basuyne noch eens hooren, | |
|   | oft in Sion yemant in ruste leyt, | |
|   | Dat sy mogen ontwaken, | |
|   | van haren slaep opstaen, | Eph.5.b.14 |
|   | dat sy haer onschult niet en maken, | |
|   | als de Heere sal comen ter wraken, | |
|   | hy sal de wederspannige slaen. | |
| 8 | O boosen aert, ghy en wilt niet hooren | |
|   | ghy maeckt u onschult alle gelijck. | |
|   | De wachters seggent u wel te vooren: | Ezec.33.a.3 |
|   | u naect de doot seer jammerlijck. | |
|   | Den vrede Gods spreect ghy en cluyten, | |
|   | maer tbloet coemt op u hooft, | |
|   | den Poortier begint te sluyten | |
|   | ende ghy sult blijven daer buyten, | |
|   | want ghy de waerheyt niet en gelooft. | |
| 9 | O Moordich zaet, wat gaet ghy maken? | |
|   | geslacht van Cain, ghi brengt ter doot | Gen.4.a.8 |
|   | Des Heeren Schaepkens sonder saken: | |
|   | twort dobbel betaelt in uwen schoot. | Apo.18.a.6 |

|   |   |   |
|---|---|---|
|   | You must set out on that narrow path,<br>A single footstep is its width.<br>Its entrance lies in humbling yourself,<br>Where your inheritance you'll receive;<br>Do not fear—though you may be frail—<br>The eagle with its mighty wings;<br>He will strike you with his claws. | Mt 7:13<br><br><br><br><br>2 Es 11 |
| 6 | The dragon has come upon the Earth,<br>And is consumed with fury great.<br>For the Woman who had borne the Man-child<br>Has been robbed from him, therefore he goes into battle<br>To make war against her seed.<br>But be of good cheer and doubt ye not!<br>Our Guide will soon come to judge,<br>To sit in judgement with his servants;<br>He will deliver them from every sorrow. | Rev 12:3<br><br><br><br><br><br><br>Jude :14 |
| 7 | O, watchers on the gates of Zion!<br>Methinks that sword is now prepared:<br>Let your Trumpets sound once more,<br>Should yet any be sleeping in Zion,<br>So that they might awaken<br>And arise up from their sleep;<br>So that they cannot plead innocence<br>When the Lord comes to wreak vengeance -<br>He will smite the obstinately rebellious! | Is 52:8, 62:6<br><br><br><br><br>Eph 5:14 |
| 8 | O, evil nature, you refuse to hear!<br>You protest your innocence, all in the same way.<br>The Watchmen have warned you well in advance,<br>You draw nigh to death so wretched;<br>You joke about the peace of God,<br>But your blood will be upon your heads!<br>The Keeper goes to close the gates,<br>And you will be left outside, excluded,<br>Because you refuse to believe the truth. | <br><br>Ezek 33:3 |
| 9 | O Murderous seed, what will you do?<br>Offspring of Cain, you put to death<br>The Lambs of the Lord, without just cause -<br>It will be doubly repaid to you! | <br>Gen 4:8<br><br>Rev 18:6 |

|    | | |
|---|---|---|
|    | De Doot coemt nu te Peerde, | Apo.6.a.8 |
|    | wy hebben u eynde gesien: | |
|    | dat Sweert gaet over de eerde, | |
|    | daer ghy mede gedoot sult werden, | |
|    | de Helle en suldy niet ontvlien. | |
| 10 | Den tijt is hier nu om te maeyen, | Apo.14.b.15 |
|    | de boosheyt heeft de overhant, | 4.Esd.5.a.2 |
|    | Daer en is schier geen plaetse om saeyen, | |
|    | dat oncruyt vervult het Lant. | Mat.13.c.25 |
|    | Den Somer is schier geleden, | |
|    | ick hoor der Trompetten gepijp, | |
|    | de spootters verachten den vrede, | |
|    | tis tijt te persse te treden, | |
|    | slaet aen u seyssen, den Oogst is rijp. | Joel3.b.13 |
| 11 | God sal de vogels een maeltijt bereyden | |
|    | te Bosra en Edom, also ick las, | |
|    | Van tvlees der Coningen en Princen beyde: | Apo.19.b.17 |
|    | haest u, ghy Vogelen, versaet u ras, | |
|    | Wilt u van des Lants heeren vleesch voeden; | |
|    | so sy deden, wort haer gedaen. | |
|    | ghy knechten des Heren, zijt vroon van moede, | |
|    | de Vogels werden versaet van haren bloede, | |
|    | dit loon sullen onse roovers ontfaen. | |
| 12 | Verblijt u nu en weest in vruechden | Apo.18.c.20 |
|    | en speelt op Herpen een nieuwe liet, | |
|    | Wilt u in onsen God verhuegen | |
|    | ghy alle, die dese wrake siet. | |
|    | De Heere coemt, om te betalen, | |
|    | te wreken ons alder bloet, | |
|    | sijn gramschap begint te dalen, | |
|    | wy verwachten de laetste scahlen: | Apo.15 |
|    | o ghy bruyt, gaet uwen bruydegom te gemoet. | Mat.25.a.6 |
| 13 | Staet op, Jerusalem, wilt u bereyden, | Esa.52.a.1 |
|    | ontfangt u trouwe, aenschout u Rijck, | |
|    | Wilt u Tenten wijt uut breyden | Esa.54.a.2 |
|    | ontfangt u kinderen alse gelijck. | |
|    | Uwen Coninc coemt, om u te bevrijden, | |
|    | sijnen loon brengt hy voor hem pleyn, | Esa.62.a.1 |

|    | Death now comes riding on horseback, | Rev 6:8 |
|----|---|---|
|    | We have seen your fate! | |
|    | The Sword is passing over the land | |
|    | With which you will be killed and slain, | |
|    | And you will not escape from Hell! | |
| 10 | The time has now come to reap, | Rev 14:15 |
|    | For evil has gained the upper hand. | 2 Es 5:2 |
|    | There's hardly a space for the sowing, | |
|    | For weeds have engulfed the entire Land. | Mt 13:25 |
|    | The Summer will soon be past, | |
|    | I hear the Trumpets piping. | |
|    | The mockers despise the peace; | |
|    | 'Tis time to tread the winepress, | |
|    | Whet your scythes, the Harvest is ripe! | Jl 3:13 |
| 11 | God will prepare a feast for carrion birds | |
|    | In Bozrah and Edom, as I have read, | |
|    | Of flesh of Kings and Princes both. | Rev 19:18 |
|    | Make haste, you winged ones, sate yourselves feverishly, | |
|    | Feed on the flesh of the rulers of the Land! | |
|    | As they have done, so will be done to them! | |
|    | You servants of the Lord, be strong in spirit! | |
|    | The Birds become sated with their blood: | |
|    | This reward shall our predators receive. | |
| 12 | Now rejoice and be exultant, | Rev 18:20 |
|    | Play on your Harps a new song! | |
|    | In our God be jubilant | |
|    | All of you who witness this revenge! | |
|    | The Lord will come to repay, | |
|    | To avenge the blood of us all. | |
|    | His wrath is descending, | |
|    | We await the bowls of final wrath, | Rev 15 |
|    | O bride, go out to meet your bridegroom! | Mt 25:6 |
| 13 | Arise, Jerusalem, and will yourself prepare! | Is 52:1 |
|    | Receive your promise, behold your Kingdom; | |
|    | Spread out wide the circle of your Tents, | Is 54:2 |
|    | Receive your children, all of them in equal measure. | |
|    | Your King is coming to set you free; | |
|    | His reward he brings before him, for all to see, | Is 62:1 |

hy sal hem in u verblijden,          Sop.3.b.17
looft hem dies teewigen tijden,
verblijt u, Sion, met Jerusalem reyn.

*Hier begint het Testament dat Anneken Esajas haren Sone bestelt heeft, den 24. dach Januarij, Anno. 1539. Des morghens te neghen uren over ghelevert, als sy haer bereyde te sterven, voor den name ende dat ghetuychenisse Jesu, ende nam daer mede oorlof aen haren Sone tot Rotterdam.*

Esaja ontfangt u Testament.
Hoort mijn Sone die onderwijsinge uus moeders, [Prov.1.a.8., 4.a.1.] opent u ooren om te hooren die reden mijns monts. Siet, ic gae huyden den wech der Propheten, Apostelen ende Martelaren, [Mat.20.c.22.] ende drincke den kelc, die sy alle gedroncken hebben. Ick gae den wech, segge ic, die Christus Jesus dat [Joan.1.a.1.] eewige Woort des Vaders, vol genaden ende waerheyts [Joa.19.b.14.], die Herder der schapen, hy dat Leven wesende, door hem selven en niet door eenen anderen gewandelt heeft, ende heeft desen kelck moeten drincken. [...]

Desen wech zijn door gheghaen de [1.Pet.2.a.9.] Conincklijke Priesteren, comende vanden opganck der Sonnen, soo in Apocalypsis staet, ende zijn ingheghaen in die tijden der eewicheden, ende hebben desen [Mat.20.c.22.] kelck moeten drincken.

Desen wech hebben getreden de dooden, die daer [Apoc.6.a.9.] liggen onder den Altaer, die daer roepen, seggende: Heere almachtige God, wanneer wildy wreken dat bloet dat daer uutgestort is? [...]

Dit is den wech, dien gewandelt hebben die [Apo.4.a.4.] vierentwintich Ouders, die daer staen voor den stoel Gods, ende werpen haer croonen ende herpen voor den Stoel des Lams op haer aensichten vallende, [...]

> He will rejoice himself in you! (?)
> Praise him for this eternally,
> Rejoice, O Zion, with Jerusalem so perfect!

## *Anna Jansz's Testament to her Son Isaiah* (EXCERPTS[1])

*Here begins the Testament which Anneken prepared for her son Isaiah on the 24<sup>th</sup> day of January in the year 1539; it was delivered at 9:00 in the morning, as she was preparing herself to die for the name of Jesus and His witness, and with it she bade farewell to her son in Rotterdam.*

Isaiah, receive your Testament.
My son, hear the instruction of your mother [Pr 1:8, 4:1], and open your ears to hear the words of my mouth. Watch, today I am traveling the path of the Prophets, Apostles, and Martyrs [Mt 20:22], and drink from the cup from which they have all tasted. I am traveling the path, I say, which Jesus Christ [Jn 1:1], the eternal Word of the Father, full of grace and truth [Jn 1:14], the Shepherd of sheep, He who is Life itself, He himself and no one else traveled, and had to drink from this Cup. [...]

The Royal High priests [1 Pet 2:9] have traveled this road, coming from the rising of the Sun, as it is written in Revelation, and have entered into the time of eternity - these, too, have had to drink this Cup [Mt 20:22].

This path have traveled the dead who lie [Rev 6:9] under the Altar, who cry out there, saying: "Lord Almighty God, when will you avenge the blood which has been shed there?" [...]

This is the path which has been traveled by the [Rev 4:4] four and twenty Elders who stand before the throne of God, and, falling down on their faces, cast their crowns and harps before the Throne of the Lamb, [...]

---

1 Anna Jansz's lengthy *Testament*, published in pamphlet form already in 1539, was included in *Het Offer* as well as in van Braght's *Bloedig Toneel* (1660) and its English translation (further literature in Packull, "Anna Jansz"). Included here are selections from the *Testament* in *Het Offer* which parallel material in the following martyr song about her; it is an interesting glimpse of the care in which the song writer for *Het Offer* incorporated what are reported to be a martyr's own words.

Desen wech hebben oock ghewandelt die gheteyckenden des Heeren, die dat [Ezech.9 a.6.] teycken Thau in haer voorhooft ontfanghen hebben, die daer vercoren zijn, uut alle gheslachten der menschen [...] ende volghen dat Lammeken nae waer het henen gaet.

Siet, alle dese hebben den [Mat.20.c.22.] kelck der bitterheyt moeten drincken, Ende alle die daer noch ontbreken aent ghetal ende vervullinge Sions, die Bruyt des Lams, [Apo.21.a.2.] welck is dat nieuwe Hierusalem, die daer van boven uut den Hemel daelt [...]

Maer waer ghy hoort, dat een arm, slecht, verstooten [Luc.12.d.32.] hoopken is, dat van de Wereldt veracht ende verworpen is, daer schickt u by. Ende daer ghy vant Cruyce hoort, daer is Christus [...]

Vreest de menschen niet, verlaet [Eccl.4.d.32.] u leven liever, eer ghy vander Waerheyt wijcket, [2.Cor.5.a.1.] Ist dat ghy u lichaem dat vander aerden ghemaect is, verliest, de Heere u Godt heeft u een beter bereydt inden Hemel.[...]

[Levi.20.a.7.] Heylighet u den Heere, mijn Soon, Heylighet alle uwe wandelinghe met die vreese uus Godts. [1.Cor.10.d.31.] Al wat ghy doet, laet zijnen Naem daer in ghepresen worden. Eert den Heere in die wercken uwer handen. Laet dat [Mat.5.b.16.] licht des Evangeliums door u lichten [Mt.5.e.43.] Hebt uwen Naesten lief, Deylt met uutgestorter vuyriger herten den [Esa.58.a.7.] hongherighen u broodt, [Mt.25.c.35.] Cleedet den naecten, ende en beydet niet, datter yet tweevout by u sy, want daer altijt zijn [Mat.26.a.10.] diet ghebreck hebben. Al wat u die Heere verleent van dat [Gen.3.b.18.] sweet uus aensichts, boven u nootdruft, dat [Psa.112 a.9.] deylt dien ghy weet die den Heere vreesen, En laet niet by u blijven tot den morghen, so sal de Heere die wercken uwer [Psa.5.b.13.] handen gebenedijen, ende zijne segheninge u tot een erffenisse geven. [...]

This path have also traveled they who are the marked ones of the Lord, who have received [Ezek 9:6] the sign of Thau on their foreheads, who have been chosen from among all generations [...] and who follow the Lamb whithersoever it goes.²

See, all of these have had to drink the [Mt 20:22] cup of bitterness, as will all those who are still lacking in the total number and the completion of Zion, the Bride of the Lamb [Rev 21:2], the new Jerusalem which will descend from up above out of Heaven [...]

But if you hear of the existence of a poor, lowly, cast-out [Lk 12:32] little company, that has been despised and rejected by the World, go join it. And where you hear of the Cross, there Christ will be [...]

Do not fear people, forsake [Sir 4:28 (?)] your life rather than departing from the Truth. [2 Cor 5:1] And if you should lose your body, which has been made of mortal clay, the Lord your God has prepared for you a better one in Heaven. [...]

[Lev 20:7] Consecrate yourself to the Lord, my Son, sanctify all your doings with the fear of your God. [1 Cor 10:31] Let his Name be praised in all that you do. Honor the Lord through the works of your hands. Let the [Mt 5:16] light of Scripture shine through you. [Mt 5:43] Love your Neighbor; with an effusive, passionate heart deal your bread to the [Is 58:7] hungry. [Mt 25:35] Clothe the naked, and do not tolerate having two of something with you, for there will always be those [Mt 26:11] who are in need of it. All that the Lord grants you in the [Gen 3:19] sweat of your brow, beyond that which you need, that [Ps 112:9] share with those whom you know fear the Lord. And do not put it off until the morrow, so the Lord will bless the works of your [Ps 5:12] hands, and will give you his blessing for an inheritance. [...]

---

2 This curious passage cites most of Rev 14:4-5, with a cryptic gloss from the sixteenth-century editor: "out of all generations of those who have not defiled themselves with women (understand this well), and who follow the lamb wherever it goes."

*Een Liedeken van Anneken van Rotterdam*

Na de wijse: Vanden 48. Psalm.
Ofte, Geen meerder vruecht ter werelt en is.

*Melody: Souterliedeken 48*

1 Een groote vruecht ist int gemeyn
  Dat douders hare kinder cleyn  Pro.22.a.6., Eccl.7.c.25,
                Eph.6.a.4.
  In Gods vreese opvoeden
  Met onderwijsing in den Heer
  Neerstich voorhoudende Gods leer
  Sparen daer toe geen roeden.  Pro.13.c.24.

2 Hoort hoe Anneken oorlof nam
  Aen haren soon te Rotterdam
  Als haer de doot aenstonde:
  Esaja ontfangt u testament
  Wilt hooren na de reden jent  Prov.1.a.8., 4.a.1.
  Die gaen uut mijnen monde.

*A Song about Anneken of Rotterdam*

To the Tune: "Of the 48th Psalm"
or "No greater joy on earth there is"

| | | |
|---|---|---|
| 1 | For the commonweal it is great joy | Pr 22:6, Sir 7:23, Eph 6:4 |
| | That parents raise their children young | |
| | In the fear of God | |
| | With admonitions in the Lord, | |
| | In diligence holding up God's precepts | |
| | And sparing not the rod. | Pr 13:24 |
| 2 | Now hear how Anneken took her leave | |
| | From her son in Rotterdam, | |
| | When death drew near to her: | |
| | "Isaiah, receive your testament, | |
| | And hear upon my words so fine, | Pr 1:8, 4:1 |
| | Which from my mouth now do depart." | |

| | | |
|---|---|---|
| 3 | Siet der Propheten wech ick gae | |
| | Apostlen Martelaren nae | |
| | Drinck mee den Kelck ter stede | Mat.20.c.22 |
| | Dien sy gedroncken hebben voor | |
| | Christus self trat desen wech door | Luc.24.c.25 |
| | Dranck oock den Kelck mede. | |
| 4 | Desen wech zijn door gepasseert | |
| | Die Coninclijcke Priesters weert | 1.Pet.2.a.9. |
| | Die vanden Oosten quamen | |
| | En zijn de tijt der eewicheyt | |
| | Ingegaen door den wech bereyt | |
| | Droncken den kelck altsamen. | |
| 5 | Sy gingen oock door desen pat | |
| | Die dooden die daer leggen plat | Apoc.6.a.9 |
| | Onder dAltaers behoede | |
| | Die roepen en seggen: O Heer | |
| | Du warachtighe Godt, wanneer | |
| | Wreect ghy uus Dienaers bloede. | |
| 6 | Hier door gaende met vroom gemoet | |
| | De vierentwintich Ouders goet | Apo.4.a.4. |
| | Staen voor den Stoel des Heeren | |
| | Sy werpen af haer Croonen fraey | |
| | Voort Lam, en hare Herpen draey | |
| | Vallen neer Godt ter eeren. | |
| 7 | Door dien wech gingen si gemeyn | |
| | Al diet teycken Thau hadden pleyn | Ezec.9.a.6., Apo.7.a.3. |
| | In haer voorhooft ontfangen | |
| | Vercoren zijnde uut alle saet | |
| | Der menschen, en so waer tLam gaet | Apo.14.a.4. |
| | Volgen sy zijne gangen. | |
| 8 | Siet dese moesten in dit dal | |
| | Drincken den bitteren Kelck al | Mat.20.c.22. |
| | En so watter noch faelde | |
| | Aent getal Syons des Lams Bruyt | |
| | Dat wort Jerusalem beduyt | Apoc.21.a.2. |
| | Die van den Hemel daelde. | |

| | | |
|---|---|---|
| 3 | "See, I tread down the Prophets' road,<br>Follow the Martyrs and Apostles,<br>In this place drink with them the Cup<br>Which they did drink before me;<br>Christ himself trod down this road,<br>And also drank the Cup with us." | Mt 20:22<br><br>Lk 24:26 |
| 4 | "This is the path which has been trod<br>By Royal High priests worthy,<br>Who came from regions in the East<br>And entered time everlasting<br>Through the way prepared for them -<br>They drank the cup together." | 1 Pet 2:9 |
| 5 | "They, too, did travel down this road<br>The dead now stretched out, lying<br>Beneath the Altar's keep;<br>They cry out loudly, call: 'O Lord!<br>You sovereign God! and when<br>Will you avenge your Servants' blood?'" | Rev 6:9 |
| 6 | "Traversing through with pious heart,<br>The four and twenty Elders good<br>Stand before the Throne of God;<br>Their beauteous Crowns they do cast off<br>Before the Lamb, and their Harps, too,<br>With haste fall down, to God's own honor." | Rev 4:4 |
| 7 | "They traveled down that road together<br>All those who had received so plainly<br>On their foreheads the sign of Thau;<br>Elected are they from all the seed<br>Of mankind, and wherever the Lamb does go<br>They follow in its footsteps." | Ezek 9:6, Rev 7:3<br><br><br>Rev 14:4 |
| 8 | "See, in this vale these had to<br>All drink the bitter Cup;<br>And whatever may have yet been missing<br>For the completion of Zion, the Bride of the Lamb,<br>That will be clarified in Jerusalem,<br>Which descended down from Heaven." | Mt 20:22<br><br><br>Rev 21:2 |

| | | |
|---|---|---|
| 9 | Waer dat ghy van een hoopken hoort | Luc.12.d.32. |
| | Arm ende slecht, gestoten voort | |
| | Van die werelt verschoven | Joan.15.b.19., 17.b.14. |
| | Daer wilt u altijt voegen by | |
| | En waer ghy hoort dat Cruyce sy | |
| | Daer is Christus van boven. | |
| 10 | Vreest geen menschen, u leven strijct | Mat.10.d.28. |
| | Eer dat ghy vander waerheyt wijct. | |
| | U lijf gemaect van eerde | |
| | Al ist dat ghy verlieset dat | Mat.10.e.39. |
| | U heeft bereyt een beter vat | |
| | God des Hemels van weerde. | |
| 11 | Heylicht u den Heere mijn soon | Levi.20.a.7. |
| | En heylicht uwe wandel schoon | |
| | Met den Heere te vresen | |
| | Eert uwen Godt aen allen cant | 1.Co.10.d.31. |
| | In al de wercken uwer hant | |
| | Sijn Naem laet zijn gepresen. | |
| 12 | Deylt me u broot die honger heeft | Esa.58.a.7., Tobi.1.c.17. |
| | Met uutgestorter herten geeft | |
| | Cleet naecten sonder toeven | |
| | Tot eeniger tijt vertrect niet | |
| | Datter tweevout by u sy yet | |
| | Altijt zijn diet behoeven. | Mat.26.b.10. |
| 13 | Al dat u die Heere toeleet | |
| | Boven nootdruft vant aensichts sweet | Gen.3.b.18. |
| | Laet Gods volc daer af leven | |
| | En verbeyt niet tot morgen toe | |
| | U werc sal God vermeeren soe | Psa.5.b.13., 115.b.13. |
| | Den segen sal hy u geven. | |
| 14 | Alsmen duysent vijfhondert jaer | |
| | Negenendertich schreef daer naer | |
| | Liet Anneken haer Leven | |
| | Sy is geweest een schoon voorbeelt | |
| | Dat welc aen veel Christenen feelt | |
| | Die haer tot God begeven. | |

FINIS.

9     "Where you hear of a little company,     Lk 12:32
Poor and simple, cast out
Rejected by the world:     Jn 15:19, 17:14
Always join yourself to them,
And where you hear the Cross is there,
There will be Christ from on high."

10     "Fear not men, lay down your life     Mt 10:28
Before you from the truth depart.
Your body, composed of mortal clay,
You might well come to lose it -     Mt 10:39
The wondrous God of Heaven
Has prepared for you a better vessel."

11     "Be consecrated to the Lord, my son,     Lev 20:7
And sanctify your walk unblemished
By the fearing of the Lord;
Honor your God from every side,     1 Cor 10:31
In all the workings of your hand,
Let His Name be praised."

12     "Deal your bread to those who hunger,     Is 58:7, Tob 1:17
Give with unreserved heart,
Clothe the naked, do not tarry;
Lengthen not the stretch of time
That you have two of anything -
Always there are those who need it."     Mt 26:11

13     "All that the Lord makes come your way,
Beyond your basic needs, by the sweat of your brow,     Gen 3:19
Let God's people live from that,
And don't postpone until the morrow.
God will increase the work of your hands,     Ps 5:12, 115:13
And he will give his blessing to you."

14     When they wrote one thousand five hundred,
And thirty-nine years behind it,
Anneken laid down her Life;
She was a wonderful example,
Of that which lacks in many Christians
Who make their way to God.

    The End

## CLAESKEN GAELEDOCHTER

*Dit is de Belijdinge van een vrouwe ghenaemt Claesken, die om tghetuychenisse Jesu Christi haer leven heeft ghelaten, Anno, 1559.*

Vrage ende antwoort tusschen den Commissarius ende Claesken.

De Commissarius vraechde my ten eersten af, na mijnen naem, waer ic van daen was, ende na mijn ouderdom, ende noch meer ander sulcke dingen.
Ten anderen vraechde hy my: Sijt ghy gedoopt?
Cla. Ja.
Com. Wie heeft u ghedoopt?
Clae. Gielis van Aken.
Com. Die verleyder, hy selfs is zijn geloove afgegaen. Hoe dede hy, doen hy u doopte?
Cla. Hy [Mat.28.c.19.] doopte my inden naem des Vaders, des Soons, ende des heyligen Geests.
Com. Waer hebt ghy den doop ontfangen?
Cla. Tot Worckom int velt.
Com. Wasser al meer volcx by?
Clae. Ja.
Com. Wat volc wast?
Cla. Tis my vergheten.
Com. Door wat oorsake quaemt ghy daer?
Cla. Het is my vergeten. Dat mocht ick beyde met der waerheyt wel seggen.
Com. Sijn u kinderen niet gedoopt?
Cla. Mijn twee jonge kinderen niet.
Com. Waerom en hebt ghy u kinderen niet laten doopen?

# CLAESKEN GAELEDOCHTER
## (drowned March 14, 1559, in Leeuwarden)

*This is the Confession of a woman named Claesken, who gave her life for the witness of Jesus Christ, in the year 1559.*

*Questions and Answers between the Commissioner and Claesken.*

The Commissioner first asked me for my name, where I was from, my age, and some more of that kind of thing.

Then he asked me: "Have you been baptized?"
Claesken: "Yes."
Commissioner: "Who baptized you?"
Claesken: "Gielis van Aken."[1]
Commissioner: "That deceiver! He has already renounced those beliefs himself. What did he do when he baptized you?"
Claesken: "He [Mt 28:19] baptized me in the name of the Father, the Son, and the Holy Ghost."
Commissioner: "Where did you receive this baptism?"
Claesken: "In the fields at Workum."[2]
Commissioner: "Were more people there?"
Claesken: "Yes."
Commissioner: "What people?"
Claesken: "I've forgotten."
Commissioner: "What was the reason you went there?"
Claesken: "I've forgotten. I am able to say that truthfully both times."[3]
Commissioner: "Haven't your children been baptized?"
Claesken: "Not my two youngest children."
Commissioner: "Why haven't you had your children baptized?"

---

[1] Gielis (Gillis, Jelis) van Aken, supporter of Menno Simons, was an early and important Anabaptist teacher; from 1549 to 1558 he is named as baptizer by at least 15 martyrs in Amsterdam and Rotterdam. Around 1555 he was disciplined (banned) by Menno and others, possibly for his beliefs about the divinity of Christ, possibly for adultery; nevertheless, he was executed for his Anabaptist beliefs in Antwerp in 1558 (S. Blaupot ten Cate, *Geschiedenis der Doopsgezinden in Holland, Zeeland, Utrecht en Gelderland*. Vol. 1 [Amsterdam: P.N. van Kampen, 1847], 21-22).

[2] A town in Friesland near the shore of what was then the Zuider Zee, now the inland body of water called the "Ijsselmeer."

[3] Claesken is making the point that though her answers are brief, they are not false; like all Anabaptists, she took seriously the Scriptural injunction against lying, regardless of the circumstances.

Claes. Om dat my daer so wel aen genoechde, sose my de Heere gegeven heeft.
Com. Waerom genoechde u aen Abraham ende Sicke so wel, ende aen Douwe niet? ghy hebt Douwe ymmers al laten doopen.
Cla. Doen wiste icket niet.
Com. Wat en wist ghy doen niet?
Cla. Dat ic nu weet.
Com. Wat weet ghy nu?
Cla. Dat de [Mat.11.d.25.] Heere my te kennen gegeven heeft.
Com. Wat heeft u de Heere te kennen gegeven?
Cla. Dat ict inde Schriftuere niet verstaen en can, dat sulcx behoort.
Com. Hoe lange en hebt ghy niet te kercken geweest?
Cla. In negen of tien Jaren niet.

Dit zijn de vragen, die hy my afghevraecht heeft, maer hy heeft veel meer woorden gehadt, ende als ick hem so geringe niet en antwoorde, so seyde hy, dat ick den stommen Duyuel in hadde, de [2.Cor. 11.b.16.] Duyvel stelde hem in een Engel des lichts in ons, soo waren wy met de Ketters altemael. Doen las hy my de Articulen voor, also ickse beleden hadde, ende seyde my: Het soude voor de heeren comen, begheerde icket, hy woudet noch wel anders schrijven. Ick seyde: Ghy en derftet niet anders schrijven.

*Vrage ende antwoort tusschen den Kettermeester ende Claesken.*

Kettermeester. Waerom hebt ghy u laten doopen?
Claesken. De Schriftuere ghetuycht van een nieu leuen. [Mat. 3.a.2.] Joannes roept ten eersten van boete, [Mat. 4.b.17.] Christus selfs oock, de [Act.2.d.38.] Apostolen na, sy leerden het volc boete ende beteringe te doen, ende dan souden sy haer laten doopen, soo hebbe ick my tot boete ende beteringe begeven, ende hebbe my laten doopen.
Daer en seyde hy niet veel tegen.
Ket. Waerom en hebt ghy u kinderen niet laten doopen?
Clae. Ick en cant inde Schriftuere niet verstaen, dat sulcx behoort.
Ket. David seyt ymmers: [Psa.51.a.7.] In sonden ben ic geboren, in sonden heeft my mijn moeder ontfangen. Daerom dat de kinderen in erfsonde geboren zijn, moetense gedoopt worden, sullen sy salich worden.

| | |
|---|---|
| Claesken: | "Because I was so well satisfied with them as the Lord had given them to me." |
| Commissioner: | "Why were you so well satisfied with Abraham and Sicke, and not with Douwe? After all, you did have Douwe baptized already." |
| Claesken: | "Then I didn't know that yet." |
| Commissioner: | "What didn't you know yet, then?" |
| Claesken: | "That which I know now." |
| Commissioner: | "What do you know now?" |
| Claesken: | "That which the [Mt 11:25] Lord has revealed to me." |
| Commissioner: | "What has the Lord revealed to you?" |
| Claesken: | "That I cannot understand from Scripture that such is right." |
| Commissioner: | "How long haven't you been in church?" |
| Claesken: | "Not for nine or ten years." |

These are the questions he posed me, but he used a lot more words. When I did not answer him as briefly, he said that I was possessed by the dumb Devil: the [2 Cor 11:14] Devil pretended to be an Angel of light in us, and so we, all of us, were heretics. Then he read back to me the Articles as I had confessed them, and told me that this would be brought before the magistrates; if I wished, he would be willing to write something different. I said: "You may not write it differently."

*Questions and Answers between the Inquisitor and Claesken* (excerpts)

| | |
|---|---|
| Inquisitor: | "Why did you have yourself baptized?" |
| Claesken: | "Scripture testifies of a new life. [Mt 3:2] John calls first for repentance, [Mt 4:17] Christ himself as well, similarly the [Acts 2:38] Apostles: they taught the people to repent and better their hearts, and only then should they have themselves baptized. Just so I turned myself to repentance and betterment of heart, and then had myself baptized." |

(He didn't say a lot to that.)

| | |
|---|---|
| Inquisitor: | "Why haven't you had your children baptized?" |
| Claesken: | "I cannot understand from Scripture that that is proper." |
| Inquisitor: | "After all, David did say: [Ps 51:7] 'In sin I was born, in sin did my mother conceive me.' Because children have been born into original sin, they must be baptized if they are to receive salvation." |

Cla. Mach een mensche salich worden door een uutwendich teecken, so is Christus te vergeefs gestorven.
Ket. Daer staet, Joan. 3. Men moet [Joan.3.a.5.] herboren wesen uut den water ende Geest, daerom moeten de kinderen oock ghedoopt zijn.
Cla. Dat spreeckt Christus niet totten kinderen, maer totten verstandighen, daerom heb ick my tot de wedergeboorte begeven, wy weten dat de kinderen in de handen des Heeren zijn. De Heere seyde: [Mt.19.b.14.] Laet de kinderen tot my comen, sulcken behoort het rijcke der Hemelen toe.
Ket. [2.Cor.1.b.14., 16.b.15.] Stephanens huysghesin worde ghedoopt, daer mochten ooc by avontueren wel kinderen mede gheweest zijn.
Claes. Wy en staan niet op het avontuer, wy hebben wel een sekere vasticheyt.
Hy en seyde daer ooc niet veel tegen. [...]

Het begin ende het eynde was dat ick den [Joan. 8.e.52.] Duyvel in hadde, ende dat ick verleyt was.
Ic seyde: Is Christus dan een verleyder?
Hy seyde: Neen, Christus en is geen verleyder.
Ick seyde: So en ben ick oock niet verleyt, ick en soecke noch begeere niet anders, dan den [Deu.6.b.18., Mat.22.d.36.] Heere van gansscher herten te vreesen, niet een tittel wetens van zijn geboden over te treden.

Als hy my dan noch langer te voren ghecalt hadde, so seyde hy dan: Ick en can nu niet anders seggen, ghy muecht u bedencken. Ic seyde: Ic en derf my niet anders bedencken, ic weet wel, dat ick de waerheyt voorhanden hebbe. Als ic dan weder voor hem quam, so seyde hy: Jae Claesken, hoe hebt ghy u bedacht? Cla. Ick heb my bedacht, dat ick begheere daer by te blyven, daer my de Heere toe geroepen heeft.
Ket. De Duyvel heeft u gheroepen, die stelt hem in een Enghel des lichts in u lieden. [...]

| | |
|---|---|
| Claesken: | "If a person can be saved through an external sign, then Christ died in vain." |
| Inquisitor: | "It says in John 3, 'One must [Jn 3:5] be born again through water and the Spirit'; and therefore children, too, must be baptized." |
| Claesken: | "Christ does not say that to children, but to those who have reached the age of discernment; this is why I have given myself to being reborn. We know that children are in the hands of the Lord. The Lord said: [Mt 19:14] 'Suffer the children to come unto me, for to such belongs the kingdom of Heaven.'" |
| Inquisitor: | "[1 Cor 1:16, 16:15] Stephen's whole household was baptized; there's a good chance that it might have included children." |
| Claesken: | "We do not build on chance, for we have a firm assurance." |

(He didn't say a lot to that, either.)

[*Under continued questioning Claesken stoutly and impressively defends her beliefs on church attendance, the sacraments, the primacy of Scripture over church tradition, the believer's right to interpret Scripture, and her continued faith despite van Aken's vacillation.*]

The long and short of it was that I was possessed by the [Jn 8:52] Devil, and that I had been deceived.

| | |
|---|---|
| I said: | "Then is Christ a deceiver?" |
| He said: | "No, Christ is not a deceiver." |
| I said: | "Well, then I'm not deceived either; I neither seek nor desire anything other than to fear the [Dt 6:18, Mt 22:37] Lord with my whole heart, and to not knowingly break even a tittle of his laws." |

When he had babbled at me even longer than before, he said: "I can say nothing more now, you ought to reconsider." I said: "I may not reconsider, I know for sure that I have the truth at hand." And when I came before him again, he said: "Well, Claesken, how have you reconsidered?" Claesken: "I have considered that I desire to remain steadfast in that to which the Lord has called me." Inquisitor: "The Devil has called you, he pretends to be an Angel of light in you people."

Doen verhoorde hy my noch eens, ende vraechde my: Ghelooft ghy noch niet, dat de Apostolen Christus vleesch aten?

Clae. Ick hebt u gheseyt.
Ket. Segghet nu.
Clae. Ick en segget u nu niet meer.
Ketter. Blijft ghy noch alleleens inden Doop?
Clae. Ghy wetet ymmers wel, datmen de [Mat.28.c.19., Mar.16.b.15.] boetveerdighe behoort te doopen.
Ket. Dat is al waer, alsser een Jode coemt, die nog niet ghedoopt en is. Blijft ghy noch alleleens inde kinderdoop?

Cla. Ja ick.
Ket. Gelooft ghy dan niet anders?
Clae. Ick en geloove niet anders dan Christus bevolen heeft.

Ketter. So ghetuyghe ick over u, dat ghy eewich inder Hellen gront moet ghequelt worden.
Claes. Hoe dorst ghy my so grouwelijcken verordeelen, daer doch het ordeel den Heere alleen toe coemt, ick en ben daer niet van verschrict, ic weet wel beter, als des Heeren dach coemt, soo salt wel anders bevonden worden.
Doen vraechde ick hem: Wat seyt mijn Man?
Kette. U Man blijft oock noch alleleens, de Heere moet u verlichten.

Clae. Wy zijn al [Mat.4.b.16.] verlicht, de Heere sy ghelooft.

Van mijnen Doop en maeckte hy niet veel woorden, noch vande kinderdoop, dan al zijn callen was, datmen Christus vleesch eten ende zijn bloet drincken moeste, ende vande Insettinge over duysent vijfhondert Jaer, ende dat ic simpel was, ende dat ic het Testament nau eens doorlesen en hadde. Ic seyde: Wat meynt ghy, dat wy opt [1.Cor.9.e.26.] onseker aenloopen? het is ons niet verborghen wat int nieuwe Testament staet. [Mat.19.d.29.] Wy verlaten ons lieve kinderen, die ic om de geheele werelt niet verlaten en woude, ende wy settent daer al by op, wat wy hebben, souden wy noch opt onseker

[*A sixth and seventh questioning focuses on the Sacraments and her beliefs concerning the literal presence of God's body in the host. Unable to convince her, the Inquisitor washes his hands of her blood and goes to relinquish her to the secular authorities. Still....*]

Then he examined me one more time, and asked me:
Inquisitor:  "Do you still refuse to believe that the Apostles ate Christ's body?"
Claesken:  "I've told you already."
Inquisitor:  "Say it now."
Claesken:  "I'm not going to tell you again."
Inquisitor:  "Do you hold fast to your beliefs about Baptism?"
Claesken:  "You know very well that one ought to baptize the [Mt 28: 19, Mk 16:16] the repentant."
Inquisitor:  "That's true, if a Jew were to come who had not yet been baptized. Do you hold just as fast to your position on infant baptism?"
Claesken:  "I certainly do."
Inquisitor:  "You don't believe something different?"
Claesken:  "I believe nothing different from what Christ has commanded."
Inquisitor:  "So I testify over you that you will be tormented eternally in the depths of Hell."
Claesken:  "How dare you condemn me so horribly, since judgement belongs to the Lord alone? That doesn't frighten me, for I know better: when the day of the Lord comes, it will likely be quite different."
Then I asked him: "What did my Husband say?"
Inquisitor:  "Your Husband has remained similarly steadfast, the Lord will have to show you the light."
Claesken:  "We have already seen the [Mt 4:16] light, the Lord be praised."

(He didn't say a lot about my baptism, nor about the baptism of infants, for all he babbled on about was that one had to eat Christ's body and drink his blood, and about the Ordinances of the last one thousand five hundred years, and that I was simpleminded, and that I had barely read through the Scripture even once. I said: "What do you think, that we are running on [1 Cor 9:26] uncertainty? What is contained in the New Testament is not hidden from us. [Mt 19:29] We forsake our beloved children, whom I would not forsake for the whole world, and we put all that we have at stake: would we then be

aenloopen, wy en soecken anders niet dan onse salicheyt, ghy en
mueghet ons ymmers met de heylighe Schrift niet bewijsen, dat wy
een tittel teghen des Heeren woort gebruycken ende gelooven. Het
was al met hem, dat wijt al vanden [Mat.10.c.25.] Duyvel hadden,
ende dat wy de hooveerdige duyvel in hadden. Ick seyde: Wy weten
dat de [Luc.1.d.48.] hooveerdige vanden stoel gestooten zijn. Hy
hadde so lange reden, dat hem somtijts als dochte, oft ic na hem
hooren woude, so moeste ic somtijts spreken, om dat ic niet hebben en
woude dat hem dat duncken soude, Ic en mochtet van hem niet hooren,
so grouwelijck als hy teghen de waerheyt sprack. [Jude.a.10., b.16.]

*Hier nae volcht eenen Brief vande voorgaende Claesken, aen hare Vrienden
nae den vleesche ende oock nae den geeste, uut der ghevanckenisse
gheschreven, int Jaer 1559. den 14. Martij, Ende is op de selfde tijt oft
daer ontrent, met haren lieven man, ende haren broeder Jacques, om
tghetuychenisse Jesu ghedoodet.*

[...] Ick moet u voorts van mijn droefenisse verhalen, die ick hadde
eer ick ghevanghen worde: Nu mercke ick op des Apostels woorden,
dat ick [2.Cor.7.a.9.] Godtlijcke druck hebbe ghehadt, ende dat die
Godlijcke rouwe tot salicheyt werckt. Jae sulcke droeffenisse hadde
ick somtijts, dat ick niet wiste waer henen, dat ick somtijts riep met
luyder stemmen totten Heere, ende seyde: [Eze.36.e.26.] O Heere
vermorselt my doch dat oude herte, ende geeft my een nieu herte,
ende gemoet, dat ick oprecht voor uwen oogen bevonden mach
worden. Ick seyde tot mijn lieve Man: Als ick mijn leven by de
scriftuere mete, so ist oft ic te gronde ghaen sal. Ick mach met David
wel segghen: [Psa.38.a.5.] Mijn sonden zijn over mijn hooft ghevaren,
ghelijck een sware last zijnse my te swaer gheworden. Ick seyde: Mijn
lieve Man, bidt doch den Heere voor my, Ick worde soo bestreden,
hoe dat ick mijn ghedachten meer nae den Heere sette, hoe dat die
tenteerder my meer met ander ghedachten aencoemt. [1 Pet.5.a.8.]
Ende soo riep ick dan totten Heere, ende seyde: O Heere ghy weet

running on uncertainty? We seek nothing but our salvation; after all, you cannot prove to us from Holy Scripture that we have acted or believed a tittle against the word of the Lord." All that he talked about was that we had it all from the [Mt 10:25] Devil, and that we had the devil of pride in us. I said: "We know that the [Lk 1:52] proud are knocked down from their thrones." He held such long speeches that he sometimes thought that I was coming to see things his way, and so sometimes I had to answer because I didn't want him to think that. I couldn't bear to listen to him, so horribly did he speak against the truth. [Jude 10:16])

*Here follows a letter from the aforementiond Claesken to her friends in body and spirit, written in prison in the year 1559, on March 14. And at that time, or close to it, she together with her beloved husband and her brother Jacques were killed for their witness of Christ* (excerpt):

[*Claesken's lengthy letter admonishes, instructs, and strengthens her friends; her biblical knowledge is extensive, her ability to formulate her thoughts in convincing prose superb. Included here is the final section which strikes a different tone, telling of the "great sadness" which she experienced before her imprisonment.*]

Further I must tell you about the great sadness I had before I was imprisoned: now I heed the Apostle's word that I [2 Cor 7:9] had a Godly sorrow, and that that Godly sorrow works for salvation. Yes, I sometimes had such deep sadness that I did not know where to turn, that sometimes I cried in a loud voice to the Lord and said: [Ezek 36:26] "O Lord, crush my old heart, and give me a new heart and mind, so that I might be found upright before your eyes." I said to my dear Husband: "If I measure my life against the Scriptures, it seems to me that I will perish. I might well say with David: [Ps 38:4] 'My sins have grown over my head, like a heavy burden they have become too heavy for me.'" I said: "My dear Husband, do pray to the Lord for me, I am so beleaguered, the more I turn my thoughts to the Lord, the more the tempter comes to me with other thoughts." [1 Pet 5:8] And so I would cry to the Lord, and say: "O Lord, you know

ymmers wel, dat ick anders niet begheere, dan u te vreesen. Mijn Man vertrooste my dan somtijts, hem dochte, ick en dede niet, ofte het mochte voor den Heere wel bestaan. Ick seyde: [Apo.2.a.4.] Ick en hebbe mijn eerste liefde niet, daerom bedroeve ick my dat ick niet slapen en can? Daer is geen hoope om die sonden te sterven, Ick sorghe lange te leven, Al sette ick my noch soo veel nae beteringe, ick blijf al even snoode, [Rom.7.c.24.] Ick ellendich mensche, waer sal ick henen?

Ick soude u wat meer gheschreven hebben, maer doen quam my de bode, dat wy reysen souden. Mijn hertgrondelijcke lieve vrienden, soo blijden sentencie hebben mijn Man ende ick, ende onse broeder ghehoort, wy bewesen elck den anderen een alsulcken liefde, ende hadden alsulcken blijden ghemoedt, Ick danckte den Heere soo grootelijck, dattet alle die heeren hoorden, Sy susten my, maer ick sprac al even vrijmoedich. Ende doen wy onse sentencie gehoordt hadden, doen spraken wy alle drie, ende seyden, dat sy dat rechtveerdige bloet veroordeelt hadden, met meer ander woorden. Mijn lieve man sprack so vriendelijck, ende seyde soo veel, Jae wy danckten den Heere met eenen blijden aensichte, dattet al tvolck aensach. [Act.20.d.30.] Hier mede wil ick u den Heere bevelen, Haest u, dat ghi by ons moecht comen, ende dat wy met malcanderen in der eewicheyt mogen leven.

*Dit is noch eenen brief ofte Belijdinge van de selfde Claesken, nu op nieu hier by geset.*

[...] Doen ick voor hem quam, begost hy van den kinderdoop, ende van mijn Doop ende van datmen Christus vleys eten moest, ende veel ander. Ick seyde: Ghy derft geen ophael beghinnen, het is my niet ghegeven met u te disputeren. Ick segghe u plat uut, ick begheere daer by te blijven, daer in de Heere my gheroepen heeft. Hy seyde: De Duyvel hadde my gheroepen. Ick seyde: Is die Duyvel nu soo van aert, dat hy dat quade afstaet, ende dat goet doet? het gaet met ons, als die Propheet seyt: [Esa.59.b.15.] Wie hem vant quaet afkeert, die moet allemans roof wesen, soo ist met ons gheghaen van den eersten dach af, dat wy onse ydele boose leven af lieten, doen worden wy van alle man gehaet, gelijc als Christus seyt, [Mat.10.c.22.] ghy sult van alle menschen om mijns Naems wille ghehaet worden. Hy seyt, [Esa.51.b.7., Mat.10.d.28.] vreest niet die ghene die dat Lichaem doodden, ende gheen macht hebben, dat sy meer moghen doen, maer vreest de ghene, die Siel ende Lichaem in die Helle verdoemen mach.

very well that I desire nothing but to fear you!" My Husband would then comfort me sometimes, it seemed to him that I did nothing that would not be able to stand before the Lord. I said: [Rev 2:4] "I have lost my first love, that's why I'm so sad that I cannot sleep. There is no hope of dying to sin; it worries me that I might live long, for no matter how much I work at betterment, I remain just as miserably low as before. [Rom 7:24] I wretched one, where shall I turn?"

I would have written you some more, but then the message came that we had to be on our way. My most heartily beloved friends, my Husband and I, and our brother, have heard such a joyful verdict, we showed such love each to the other, and had such a joyful spirit, I thanked the Lord so passionately that all the magistrates heard it. They shushed me, but I spoke just as freely. And when we had heard the verdict, all three of us spoke, saying that they had condemned innocent blood, though with more and different words. My dear Husband spoke so gently, and said so much; yes indeed, we thanked the Lord with glad countenance, so that all the people saw it. [Acts 20:32] With this I want to commend you to the Lord; hasten yourselves, that you may come to us, and that we may live together in eternity.

*This is yet another Letter or Confession from that same Claesken added here for the first time* (excerpts):

[...] When I came before him [*the Procurer General of the Council*] he began with the baptism of infants, and about my baptism, and that one should eat the flesh of Christ, and much more. I said: "You don't have to start again, it isn't given to me to dispute with you. I say to you as plainly as possible: I desire to remain steadfast in that to which the Lord has called me." He said the Devil had called me. I said: "Well, and is the Devil now of such nature that he leaves evil and does good? It befalls us as the Prophet said: [Is 59:15] 'Whoever turns himself from evil shall become everyone's prey'; that's how it's been with us right from the very first day that we turned away from our vain and wicked lives, then we became hated by everyone, just as Christ said: [Mt 10:22] 'For my name's sake you shall be hated by all men.' He also said: [Is 51:7, Mt 10:28] 'Fear not those who kill the body, for they have no power to do more; rather fear him who may destroy both Soul and Body in Hell.' Indeed, only him

Jae die vreesen wy alleen. Hy woudet al hebben, ick soude hem segghen van die Kinderdoop, ende van Christus vleysch te eten. Ick seyde: Het en is niet weerdich, dat ick u antwoort gheve op u vraghen, so onnut vraecht ghy, Ick hebbet u ghenoech gheseyt. [...]

Hem mochtmen soo veel niet segghen, hy hielt zijn oude veers. Onse broeder haddet hem van allen dinghen soo claer bewesen met de Schriftuer, dat hy daer niet een tittel wiste teghen te seggen, Onse broeder sprack so luyde, op dat die daer van buyten aen die Cancelrye stonden, dat zijt hooren souden, hoe recht dat hijt hem bewees. Ende ick sprac oock so luyde, als ick mocht, met een blijde ghemoet, wat my de Heere in den sin gaf, dat sprack ick sonder schromen, dat al te lanc soude vallen om te verhalen. [...]

Ende als wy onse reden gheeyndicht hadden, doen vraechde ick hem, wat mijn man seyde. Hy seyde: mijn man bleef ooc alleleens. Ic seyde: Wat wilt ghy doch met mijn arme man doen, die doch niet een letter lesen en can? Doen seyde hy: Ghy sult noch meerder verdoemenisse hebben dan u man, om dat ghy lesen cont, ende hem verleyt hebt, Daermede scheyde ick van hem.

do we fear." He kept on insisting that I tell him about the baptism of infants, and about eating the body of Christ. I said: "It is not worth my while to answer your questions, you ask so wrongly. I have told you enough, I will tell you no more, we have talked about this enough."[...]

No matter how much he was told, he kept singing the same old tunes. Our brother had proven everything to him so clearly from Scripture, that he couldn't come up with even a tittle as counter argument. Our brother spoke very loudly, so that those who stood outside the Chancellery should hear how justly he proved it to him. And I also spoke as loudly as I could, with a joyful heart; I spoke without fear whatever the Lord gave into my mind, it would be too long to tell all of it. [...]

When we had finished our debate I asked him what my husband had said. He said my husband had also remained steadfast. I said, "What do you want with my poor husband, who after all can't read a single letter?" Then he said: "You will suffer greater damnation than your husband, because you can read, and you have led him astray." And with that I left him.

## Een Liedeken van Claesken
Na de wijse: Een Liedeken met vruechden ghoet.

Een Lie-de-ken met vreuch-den goet Ver-ha-len
wy met san - gen Van die vroom vrou-we
Claes - ken soet De wel-cke in voor-tij - den
lach ge - van - gen Te Leeu-wer-den ter
stadt Sy quam voor die so-phis - ten
Daer dIn-qui-si - teur sat Die na ha-ren gront visten Maer sy be-leedt de waar-heyt plat Liet
haer niet van-gen met be-droch of lis - ten.

*Melody: Souterliedeken 72*

# CLAESKEN GAELEDOCHTER

## *A Song about Claesken*
### To the Tune: "A Song with Joyfulness so Good"[4]

1    A Song with joyfulness so good
We want to tell with singing,
Of Claesken, that woman sweet and brave,
Who lay imprisoned in past times,
In Leeuwarden, in that city.
She appeared before the Sophists,    Mk 13:9, Lk 21:12
Where the Inquisitor did sit;
They questioned her faith's very foundation,
But she confessed the truth so plainly,
Was not to be caught with tricks and lies.

---

[4] Note that the melody reference is the same as the first line of the song: sometimes contrafacts (texts written to existing melodies) did use the original song's first line but then continued with a different text.

## Een Liedeken van Claesken
Na de wijse: Een Liedeken met vruechden ghoet.

1    Een Liedeken met vreuchden goet
Verhalen wy met sangen
Van die vroom vrouwe Claesken soet
De welcke in voortijden lach gevangen
Te Leeuwerden ter stadt
Sy quam voor die Sophisten    Marc.13.b.9., Luc.21.b.11.
Daer dInquisiteur sat
Die na haren gront visten
Maer sy beleedt de waarheyt plat
Liet haer niet vangen met bedroch of listen.

2    Na haren doop heeft hy getaelt
Sy heeft sonder te buygen
De schrift vrymoedelijc verhaelt
Dat van een nieu leven en boete tuygen
Johannes en Christus claer
Boet eerst den volck aenwesen    Mat.3.a.2., 4.b.17.,
                                          Marc.1.a.4., b.15.
Ooc dApostelsche schaer
En dan den doop gepresen    Mat.28.c.19.
Souden sy ontfangen daer naer
Dus had sy gedaen na de leer van desen.

3    Gelooft ghy oock dat Christus Godts Soon    Kett.
Int broot coemt doort sacreren
Neen, want hy sidt in sVaders troon    Claes. Mar.16.c. 19,
                                          Act.7.g.55.
In tanden om verteren
En coemt hy nemmermeer
Blijft ghy also gelooven    Kett.
Ghy moet ter hellen neer
Eewich van Godt verschoven
En dit is aller ketters leer
Ghy zijt verleyt, voort sprac hi daer en boven.

4    Als Christus met dApostlen at
Lieflijck zijn Avontmaele
Sijn vleysch gaf hy haer niet teten dat

## A Song about Claesken
### To the Tune: "A Song with Joyfulness so Good"[4]

1. A Song with joyfulness so good
   We want to tell with singing,
   Of Claesken, that woman sweet and brave,
   Who lay imprisoned in past times,
   In Leeuwarden, in that city.
   She appeared before the Sophists,     Mk 13:9, Lk 21:12
   Where the Inquisitor did sit;
   They questioned her faith's very foundation,
   But she confessed the truth so plainly,
   Was not to be caught with tricks and lies.

2. About her baptism he did question;
   But she, without alt'ring her course,
   Courageously the Scriptures told:
   That of new life and repentance
   Both John and Christ most clearly tell;
   'Repentance first!' was taught the people     Mt 3:2, 4:17,
                                                                         Mk 1:4, 15
   By the Apostolic host as well;
   And only then that baptism blest     Mt 28:19
   After that they should receive:
   Thus had she done, according to their teaching.

3. "Believe you, too, that Christ, God's Son,     Inq.
   Enters the bread through consecration?"
   "No, for on his Father's throne he sits;     Clae. Mk 16:19,
                                                                   Acts 7:55
   To be consumed, chewed by our teeth,
   He will not come, no never."
   "If you remain in this belief,     Inq.
   You'll go down straight to hell,
   Eternally by God rejected.
   Heretics teach this, all of them,
   You've been deceived!" He also added further:

4. "When Christ with his Apostles ate,
   So sweetly that Last Supper,
   Did he not give his flesh to eat,

En zijn bloet te drincken int generale?
Hy gafse broot en wijn　　　　　　Claes. Mat.26.c.25.,
　　　　　　　　　　　　　　　　1.Cor.11.c.23.
Maer tlichaem tot bevryen
Heeft dus d'Avontmael fijn
Hier ghelaten ons lyen
Dat wy sullen ghedachtich zijn
Sijnen bitteren doot tot elcken tyen.

5   Claesken creech de mare subijt
    Dat sy van aerdt soud scheyden
    Doen was sy also seer verblijt
    Dat sy die groote blijschap moest verbreyden
    Want sy by haer alleyn
    Alsulcx niet mocht behouwen
    Maer gaft te kennen pleyn
    Met schrift uut goeder trouwen
    Haer vrienden van beyde ghemeyn
    Naden vleysch, en die geestelijcken bouwen.

6   Sy danckte so grootlijck den Heer
    Dat al die heeren hoorden
    Sy susten haer, maer even seer
    Riep sy, en sprac vrymoedich met claer woorden
    Over trechtveerdich bloet　　　Susan.f.49., Jaco.5.a.6.
    Hebt ghy oordeel ghegheven
    Haer man sprack oock seer soet
    En Jacques daer beneven
    Al was bereyt die watervloet
    Men sach aen allen gheen schromen noch beven.

7   Inden vijftienhondertsten Jaer
    Daer toe vijftich en negen
    Sijn dees lieve Schapen eenpaer
    Te Leeuwerden een Stadt in Vrieslandt gheleghen
    Inden water verdrenct
    En schandelijck versteecken
    Maer Godt zijn volck ghedenct
    Die op zijn tijt sal wreecken　　Deu.32.e.35., Rom.12.c.19.
    Sijn uutvercoren hier ghecrenct
    O menschen vreest God, hout op van ghebreecken.
    　　　　　　　　　　　　　　　　　4.Esdr.16.g.68.

His blood to drink, by one and all?"
"He did give them bread and wine,    Clae. Mt 26:26,
                                     1 Cor 11:23
But his body for our freedom;
And thus the Last Supper so fine
He left behind for us, his people,
That we should in remembrance be
Of his bitter death, forevermore."

5   Claesken soon received the news
    That from this earth she would be parting;
    At that was she so overjoyed,
    She had to spread that great joy 'round.
    For to herself, for her alone,
    She didn't want to keep it;
    But rather made it known right plain
    Through writing, in good faith,
    To both the sorts of friends she had,
    Friends of the flesh, and friends of faith.

6   She so greatly thanked the Lord
    That all the magistrates did hear her;
    They shushed her, but despite of that
    She called out, spoke with clear words freely:
    "Over righteous blood it is              Sus 49, Jas 5:6
    That you have passed your judgement!"
    Her husband, too, spoke very kindly,
    As did Jacques, in addition.
    Though the great flood had been prepared,
    Trembling nor fear could be seen in any.

7   In the fifteen hundredth year,
    Adding another fifty-nine,
    These dearest Sheep, one of heart,
    In Leeuwarden, a Frisian City,
    Were in the water drowned
    And shamefully disposed of.
    But God his people does remember,
    And in his time he will avenge          Dt 32:35, Rom 12:19
    His chosen own, here so mistreated.
    O people! fear God, sin no more!
                                            2 Esd 16:67

# LIJSKEN DIRCKS

*Hier Volghet noch eenen Brief van Jeronimus Segersz aen zijn Huysvrou.*

Genade, vrede, vruechde van herten, door die bekentenisse Jesu Christi sy met u mijn lieve huysvrouwe Lijsken inden Heere. Ick wunsche u mijn lieve Huysvrouwe Lijsken een vyerige liefde tot God, ende een vrolijck gemoet in Christo Jesu. Weet dat ick uwer [Rom.1.a.5.] gedencke dach ende nacht in mijn ghebedt, smeeckende ende suchtende tot Godt voor u, Want ick al bedroeft ben, om uwent wille, om dat ghy daer so lange sult moeten sitten, ende wilde wel, waert des Heeren wil geweest, dat ghy uten banden geweest hadt, maer nu hevet des Heeren wille anders geweest, om dat hy u proeven wil, ende zijn cracht ende sercheyt aen u openbaren, tegen alle die tegen die waerheyt staen. Aldus en can ick tegen des Heeren wille niet gedoen, op dat ick hem niet en tenteere, dan ick wil hem veel meer loven ende dancken, dat hy ons beyde [Act.5.e.42.] weerdich ghemaeckt heeft om zijnen naem te lijden, want het zijn al te uutvercoren Schaepkens, die hy daer toe vercoren heeft, want hy heeftse [Apo.14.a.4.] ghecocht uten menschen tot eerstelingen Gods.

Ende voort mijn alderliefste, soo hebbe ick tot deser hueren seer vrolijck gheweest, den Heere loovende ende danckende, dat hy ons hier toe bequaem gemaect heeft, Maer als ick hoorde van u dat ghy meer bedroeft waert dan uwen mont gespreken conste, dat welcke my menigen traen heeft doen weenen, ende een bedroeft herte om hebbe, want het is een groote droefheyt, Ende verstont dattet soude wesen, om dat ghy my dickwils gheseyt sout hebben om van Assverus te gaen, ende dat ickt niet gedaen en hebbe, dat welcke my menigen traen gecost heeft, ende hertelijcken leedt is, [Rom.9.c.19.] nochtans en can ick tegen des Heeren wille niet gedoen, ende haddet zijnen wille geweest, hy soude ons wel een uutcoemst gegeven hebben, Maer hy heeft ons [Job.14.a.5.] mate ghestelt, ende en sullen daer niet over gaen. Aldus en connen wy den Heere niet [Tobi.13.a.2.] ont-loopen, Daerom en laet ons niet bedroeft zijn om dat werck des Heeren, maer veel meer (als [Mat.5 a.12.] Christus seyt) ons verblijden ende vrolijck zijn. [...]

# LIJSKEN DIRCKS
## (drowned February 19, 1552 in Antwerp)

*Here Follows another Letter from Jeronimus Segersz to his Wife* (excerpts):

Grace, peace, a joyful heart, through the confession of Jesus Christ, be with you, my dear wife Lijsken in the Lord. I wish you, my dear Wife Lijsken, a passionate love for God, and a joyful spirit in Christ Jesus. Know that I remember you [Rom 1:9] day and night in my prayers, beseeching and sighing to God on your behalf; I am in great sorrow on your account because you will have to be imprisoned there for such a long time. I would have wished, had it been the Lord's will, that you would have been out of your bonds, but now the Lord's will was different, because he wants to test you, and to reveal his power and might through you, against all those who stand against truth. Therefore I cannot go against the Lord's will, so that I might not tempt him, but rather I will praise and thank him all the more because he has made us both [Acts 5:41] worthy to suffer for his name; for those whom he has chosen for that are all especially selected Lambs, for he has [Rev 14:4] redeemed them from among mortals as the first fruits of God.

Further, my dearest one, therefore I have been very joyful up to this time, thanking and praising God, that he has made us fitting for this. But when I heard from you that you were more sorrowful than your tongue could express, that caused me to shed many a tear, and to have a downcast heart, for that is a great sorrow. I also understood that this might be so because you had told me so often to stop heeding Assverus,[1] and I didn't do that; this has caused me many a tear, and I am very sorry about it. [Rom 9:19] Still, I can do nothing against the will of God, and if it had been his will, he would have given us a way out. But he has given us [Job 14:5] our measure, and we will not exceed it. Hence we cannot escape [Tob 13:2] from the Lord. Therefore let us not be sad because of the workings of the Lord, but much rather (as [Mt 5:12] Christ says) rejoice and be glad. [...]

---

[1] Assverus van Gheemont, silversmith and likely a leader among the Anabaptists, was arrested with Jeronimus and Hendrik Beverts, but executed only on January 22, 1552; he allegedly confessed under torture to the names of those he had baptized (Cramer, *Het Offer*, pp. 152, 184). Not surprisingly, he was not canonized in the *Martyrs' Mirror*.

Aldus bidde ick u mijn Lief, dat ghy doch niet meer droeve en zijt, want de Heere sal u bewaren als den [Sac.2.a.8.] appel van zijnder oogen, Ja [Esa. 49. b. 15.] al waert dat een moeder haer kint vergate, so en sal ic u niet vergeten, seyt de Heere, Ja [Joa.10.c.27.] mijn schaepkens hooren mijn stemme (seyt de Heere) ende sy volghen my nae, ende niemant en salse uut mijnder hant ontnemen, Daerom mijn alderliefste, weest doch te vreden, ende betrout den Heere, [Hebr.13.a.5.] hy en sal u niet verlaten. Ende noch verstont ick eensdeels van mijn suster, dat ghy oock bedroeft waert, om dat ghy my niet meer en verdroecht, Siet mijn lieve schaep ghi en hebt my niet tegenspannich geweest, ende wy en hebben met malcanderen anders niet gheleeft, dan wy schuldich en waren te leven, waerom wildy dan bedroeft wesen? Weest doch te vreden, want Christus en sal u daer af niet reeckenen, [Ezec.18.c.21.] want hy en wil onse sonden niet gedencken. Ende ick dancke den Heere, dat ghy noch so oot-moedelijc met my geleeft hebt, Ende wilde wel, dat ic voor u mocht sitten een jaer lanck te water ende te broode, Ja en dan noch thienmael den doot mocht sterven, ende dat ghy verlost waert. Och mocht ic u helpen met mijnen tranen, ende met mijnen bloede, hoe gewillich soude ic voor u lijden, mer mijn lijden en can u niet helpen. Aldus weest doch te vreden, Ic wil den Heere noch meer voor u bidden. Ende desen brief hebbe ic met tranen geschreven, om dat ick hoorde, dat ghy so seer bedroeft zijt, Ende ick bidde u, wilt my schrijven hoe dat het met u staet. Hier mede beveel ick u den Heere.

*Dit is eenen Brief van Lijsken, Jeronimus Huysvrouwe, die sy aen hem schreef inder gevanckenisse tot Antwerpen. Anno. 1551.*

[...] Mijnen lieven Man inden Heere, de welcken ick ghetrout hebbe voor God ende zijn gemeente, den welcken si seggen, dat ic daerby in overspel geseten hebbe, om dat ic inden Baal niet getrout en ben. Maer de Heere seyt: [Mat.5.a.12.] Verblijdt u als alle menschen quaet van u seggen om mijns Naems wille, dan verblijdt ende verhuecht u, want het sal u wel geloont worden inden Hemel.

Wetet dat ick seer gheweent hebbe, om dat ghi bedroeft waert om mijnent wille, omdat ghy ghehoort hadt, dat ick u dicwils gheseyt soude hebben, om van Assverus te gaen woonen, ende dat ghy dat niet gedaen en hebt, weest daer in te vreden, mijn alderliefste in den Heere, haddet den Heere so niet belieft, ten ware so niet geschiet, [Mat.6.b.10.] des Heeren wille moet geschien tot onser beyder sielen salicheyt, want hy ons niet en laet [1.Cor.10.b.13.] becoren boven ons vermoghen. Daeromme weest

So I beseech you, my love, that you should not be sad any longer, for the Lord will keep you as the [Zech 2:8] apple of his eye; yes, [Is 49:15] "as little as a mother might forget her suckling child, so I will not forget you," says the Lord; yes, [Joh 10:27] "my sheep hear my voice," (says the Lord), "and they follow me, and no one shall take them from my hand." Therefore, my very dearest, be content, and trust in the Lord, and [Heb 13:5] he will not forsake you. I also understood, partly from my sister, that you were also sad because you had not been more tolerant towards me. Listen, my dear lamb, you were not antagonistic towards me, and we lived with one another no differently than we were obliged to live, why would you then be sad? Be satisfied, for Christ will not count it against you, [Ezek 18:22] for he will not remember our sins. And I thank the Lord that you did live so submissively with me; I would be gladly imprisoned instead of you for a year on water and bread, indeed, and then would gladly die tenfold, if you were released. O, if only I could help you with my tears, and with my blood, how willingly would I suffer for you! but my suffering cannot help you. Therefore be at peace, I will beseech the Lord even more for you. I wrote this letter in tears, because I had heard that you were so sad. And I ask you to write me about how things are going with you. With this I commend you to the Lord.

*This is a Letter from Lijsken, Jeronimus's wife, which she wrote to him in the prison in Antwerp, 1551* (excerpts):

[...] My dear Husband in the Lord, whom I married before God and his congregation, about which they say that I have committed adultery because I was not married in Baal's temple. But the Lord says: [Mt 5:12] "Rejoice when everyone speaks evil of you for my name's sake, then rejoice and be glad, for you will be rewarded in heaven."

Know that I cried a great deal because you were sad on account of me, because you had heard that I had so often said to you that you should forsake Assverus and you didn't do that; rest your mind about that, my dearest in the Lord, if the Lord had not wanted it so, it would not have happened thus. [Mt 6:10] For the Lord's will must be done for the salvation of both our souls, for he does not let [1 Cor 10:13] us be tempted beyond our ability to endure. Therefore be comforted,

getroost mijn alderliefste in den Heere, ende verblijt u inden Heere, so ghy van te vooren ghedaen hebt, hem lovende ende danckende, dat hy ons soo uutvercoren heeft, dat wy om zijns naems wille so lange mogen in banden ligghen, ende daer toe [Act.5 e.42.] weerdich bevonden zijn, hy weet wat hi daer in voorsien heeft, Al laghen die kinderen van [Num.14.a.8.] Israel langhe in der woestijne, hadden sy des Heeren stemme gehoorsaem gheweest, sy souden oock wel met Josua ende Caleb in dat Landt van Beloften ghecomen hebben. Also wy nu ooc hier inder woestijnen onder dese verslindende dieren, die haer [Psa.15.a.7., 57.b.7.] netten dagelijcs uutspreyden, om ons daer mede te vanghen, maer de Heere die soo crachtich is, ende de zijne niet en verlaet, die op hem betrouwen die bewaert hy van alle quade, Ja als den [Zach.2.a.8.] appel van zijnder oogen. So laet ons dan te vreden zijn in hem, ende ons cruys met blijschap ende met lijdtsaemheyt op ons nemen, ende verwachten met vasten betrouwen op die beloften, die hy ons [Apo.2.3.21.] belooft heeft, daer aen niet twijfelende, want hy ghetrouwe is diese beloeft heeft. op dat wi op [4.Es.2.e.41., Apo.7.b.9.] Sions berch gecroont muegen worden, ende met palmen verciert zijn, ende dat [Ap.14.a.4.] Lammeken mogen navolgen. Ick bidde u mijn lief inden Heere, weest ghetroost inden Heere, met allen lieven vrienden, Ende [1.Tess.5.c.25.] bidt den Heere voor my. Amen.

*Hier volcht noch eenen Brief van Jeronimus Segersz aen zijn Huysvrouwe.*

[...] Ick wunsche mijn beminde Huysvrouwe, die ick voor Godt ende zijn heylighe Ghemeente [1.Cor.7.a.2.] ghetrout hebbe voor mijn eyghen huysvrouwe, ghelijck als [Gen.11.c.29.] Abraham Sara, ende [Ge.24.b.15.] Isaac Rebecca, ende [Tob.7.c.14.] Tobias zijn Ooms dochter tot een huysvrouwe genomen heeft, alsoo hebbe ick u oock tot een huysvrouwe genomen, [1.Cor.7.a.2., Mat.19.a.7.] na luydt van Gods woordt ende bevel, ende niet ghelijck dese erge blinde werelt, om welcker saken wille dat ic den Heere nacht ende dach love ende dancke, dat hy ons so lange spaerde tot dien dat wi malcanderen tot een deel kenden, ende dat wy de kennisse der waerheyt ghehadt hebben, Om deser saken wille seggen sy, dat wy in overspel geseten hebben, om dat wi met dat afgodissche, vleeschelicke, ijdele, hoveerdige gulsige wesen, ende met dat overspelige gheslachte niet te samen gegeven en zijn, dat welcke niet dan eenen gruwel en is voor den oogen Gods, Daerom beliegen sy ons, gelijck sy [Mat.11.c.17.] Christum belogen hebben. Ende of sy noch seyden, dat ghy u met

my dearest in the Lord, and rejoice in the Lord as you have done from the beginning, praising and thanking him that he has so specially chosen us that we may be imprisoned for so long for his name's sake, and were found worthy for that [Acts 5:41], he knows what he foresaw with that. Although the children of [Num 14:8] Israel languished long in the wilderness, if they had obeyed the voice of the Lord, they too would have entered the Promised Land with Joshua and Caleb. Just so also we are now in the wilderness among these devouring animals who daily spread their [Ps 7:15, 57:6] nets to catch us with them. But the Lord who is so mighty, and who does not forsake his own who trust in him, those he will keep from all evil, yes, as the [Zech 2:8] apple of his eye. Therefore let us then be at peace in him, and take on our cross with joy and patience, and await with firm faith those promises which he has made us [Rev 2:3], not doubting them, for he is faithful who has promised it. This is so we might be crowned on [2 Esd 2:42, Rev 7:9] Zion's mountain, and be adorned with palms, and might follow the [Rev 14:4] Lamb. I pray you, my love in the Lord, be comforted in the Lord, with all the beloved friends, and [1 Th 5:25] pray to the Lord for me. Amen.

*Here follows yet another Letter from Jeronimus Segersz to his Wife* (excerpts):

[...] I wish my beloved Wife, whom I married before God and his holy Congregation [1 Cor 7:2] as my own wife, just as [Gen 11:29] Abraham took Sara, and [Gen 24:15] Isaac Rebecca, and [Tob 7:14] Tobias his uncle's daughter as his wife, exactly so I took you, too, as my wife, [1 Cor 7:2, Mt 19:5] according to God's word and command, and not like this horribly blind world. On account of this I praise and thank the Lord night and day, that he spared us so long that we could get to know one another a little, and that we have had knowledge of the truth. Because of this they say that we have lived in adultry, because we were not joined in that idolatrous, mortal, vain, proud, gluttonous institution, and with that adulterous generation, which is nothing but an abomination before the eyes of God. That's why they lie about us, just as they lied about [Mt 11:19] Christ. And even if they said that you should tend to your sewing,

uwen naet moeyen sout, dat en hindert ons niet, [Mat.11.c.28.] want Christus heeft ons allen geroepen, [Joa.5.d.39.] ende de schrift doen ondersoecken, want sy van hem getuycht, ende noch seyde Christus, dat Magdalena [Luc.10.d.42.] dat beste deel vercooren hadde, om dat sy de Schriftuere ondersocht. [...]

Ende voort so laet ick u weten, mijn beminde Huysvrouwe in den Heere, dat my leedt is dat ghy geweent hebt, want doen ic hoorde dat ghy beproeft waert, so hebbe ic den Heere te vyeriger nacht ende dach gebeden voor u, ende weet vastelijc, dat hy u bewaren sal, als den[Sach.2.a.8.] appel van zijnder oogen, ende ick love den Heere altijt, dat hy ons beyde [Act.5.e.42.] weerdich gemaect heeft, om zijns Naems wille te lijden, waerom dat ick seer verblijt ben. Ende doen ick uwen Brief las, ende hoorde hoet met u stont, ende dat ghy my den ghecruysten Christum wenschte tot eender groete, so spranc mijn herte ende mijnen gheest op in mijn lichaem van blijschappen. Ja alsoo, dat ick den Brief niet geheel uut gelesen en conde, ic en moeste mijn [Eph.3.b.14.] knien buygen voor den Heere, ende hem loven ende dancken van zijnder sterckheyt, troost ende blijschap, hoe wel dat ick nochtans bedroeft was om onse Broeders wille, ende om uwent wille, dat ghy daer so lange sult moeten sitten. Ic hebbe u den Heere in zijnen handen bevolen met de vrucht, ende betrouwe hem dat, ende en twijfele daer niet aen, hy en sal u de selve blijschap gheven, die hy my gheeft, ende sal u [1.Pet.1.a.5.] bewaren tot den eynde toe. [...]

*Noch eenen Brief van Lijsken, Jeronimus Huysvrouwe.*

[...] Ick en can den Heere niet te vollen gedancken noch gheloven [Eccl.43.d.43.] van de groote ghenade, ende vande grondeloose bermherticheyt ende van de groote Liefde, die hy aen ons bewesen heeft, dat wy zijn [2.Cor.6.c.17.] sonen ende dochteren souden zijn, ist dat wy verwinnen, [Apo.3.c.21.] gelijck hy verwonnen heeft. Och te recht mogen wy wel seggen, [Hebr.11.a.2.] dat het oprecht geloove hem schict na het gene dat niet en schijnt dat welcke [Gala.5.a.6.] door de liefde werckende is, dat welcke ons tot heerlijcheyt brengen sal, [Rom.8.b.17.] ist anders dat wy met hem lijden. Laet ons bemercken lieve Vrienden inden Heere, hoe groote liefde dat de wereltlijcke menschen hebben deen tegen den anderen. Daer zijnder (by hooren seggen) op den Steen, die haer verblijden als sy ter pijnbanck gaen souden, om de gene wille, die sy lief hebben, dat syse dan te naerder souden zijn, hoe wel dat sy in persoone by malcanderen niet en mochten comen. Hoort doch mijn beminde Broeders ende Susters inden Heere, heeft de werelt alsulcke liefde, och wat liefde behooren wy dan te hebben,

that will not deter us, [Mt 11:28] for Christ has called all of us, [Jn 5:39] and led us to search Scripture, for it testifies of him. Further, Christ said that Mary [Lk 10:42] had chosen the best part, because she searched Scripture [...]

And further I am letting you know, my beloved Wife in the Lord, that I am sorry that you cried, for when I heard that you were being questioned, I prayed to the Lord day and night all the more passionately for you. Know for certain that he will keep you as the [Zech 2:8] apple of his eye. I praise the Lord always, that he has made us both [Acts 5:41] worthy to suffer for his name's sake, for which reason I rejoice greatly. And when I read your Letter, and heard how things were with you, and that as a greeting you wished me the crucified Christ, so my heart and my soul sprang in my body for joy. Yes, so much so, that I could not finish the letter completely, I had to fall to my [Eph 3:14] knees before the Lord, and praise and thank him for his might, comfort, and joy, even though I was still sorrowful because of our Brethren, and for your sake, that you will have to be imprisoned there for so long. I have commended you to the hands of the Lord together with the fruit of your womb; trust him, and do not doubt that he will give you the same joy that he gives me, and will keep you [1 Pet 1:5] to the very end.

*Another letter from Lijsken, Jeronimus's Wife* (to friends and to her husband: excerpts):

[...] I cannot thank nor praise the Lord enough [Sir 43:27] for the wonderful grace and for the endless mercy, and for the great Love which he has shown to us, so that we might be his [2 Cor 6:18] sons and daughters if we overcome [Rev 3:2] just as he overcame. Oh, truly, we might well say [Heb 11:1] that upright faith reconciles itself to that which is not seen, [Gal 5:6] that which is working through love, that which shall bring us to glory, [Rom 8:17] provided that we suffer with him. Let us note, beloved Friends in the Lord, how great a love worldly people have one for another. There are those in the Steen[2] (it's been said), who rejoice when they are brought to the rack, because of those whom they love, so that they can be closer to them even though they cannot come together in person. Do hear, my beloved Brothers and Sisters in the Lord, if the world has such love, oh, what love ought we then to have, who are expectant of

---

[2] Antwerp's main prison, where the majority of Anabaptists were executed.

die so schoone beloften verwachtende zijn. Ick sie noch een schoon ghelijckenisse voor ooghen, van een Bruyt, hoe sy haer verciert om haren Bruydegom deser werelt te behaghen. Och hoe behooren wy ons dan te vercieren, om onsen Bruydegom te behagen. [...] Ick bidde den Heere nacht ende dach, dat hy ons alsulcken bernende liefde wil geven, dat wy niet aen en sien wat tormenten sy ons aendoen moghen. [...] Weet mijnen lieven Man inden Heere, doen ick las dat ghy soo seer verblijt zijt inden Heere, soo en mocht ick den Brief niet uut gelesen, ick en moeste den Heere bidden, dat hy my oock de selve blijschap wilde geven, ende behouden totten eynde toe, opdat wy met vruechden onse offerande doen moghen tot prijs van onsen [Mat.6.b.9.] Vader die inden Hemel is, ende tot stichtinge van allen lieven broeders ende susters. [Act.20.d.32.] Hier mede wil ic u den Heere bevelen, ende dat woort zijnder genaden. Weet dat ic u seer dancke van uwen Brief, die ghy my gheschreven hebt. De ghenade des Heeren sy met ons altijt.

*Noch eenen Brief van Lijsken gheschreven aen haren Man.*

[...] Ick wensche ons tween, den gecruysten Christum tot eenen Beschermer ende Behoeder van onser Sielen. Den selven wil ons bewaren in alle gherechticheyt, heylicheyt, ende waerheyt tot den eynde toe, ende hy sal ons oock bewaren als zijn sonen ende dochteren, ist dat wy behouden de [Heb.3.b.14.] Godsdiensticheyt zijns wesens tot den eynde toe, Ja als den [Zach.2.a.8.] appel van zijnder ooghen. Hierom so laet ons hem betrouwen, ende hy en sal ons inder eewicheyt niet [Heb.13.a.5.] verlaten, maer sal ons bewaren, als hy de zijne van het begintsel der werelt gedaen heeft, ende en [1.Cor.10.b.13.] laet ons niet met eenige tentacie bevangen, dan die menschelijck zijn. De Heere is getrouwe (seyt Paulus) die en sal ons niet laten becoren boven ons vermoghen. [2.Cor.1.a.3.] Gedanct sy God de Vader ons Heeren Jesu Christi, die ons hier toe [Act. 5. e. 42.] bequaem gemaect heeft, om zijnen naem een cort verganckelijc lijden te lijden, voor so schoone beloften, die hy ons beloeft heeft, met alle den genen die daer volstandich blijven in zijnder leere, ende [Sap.3.a.] in weynich mogen wy hier lijden, maer in velen sullen wy geloont worden.

Mijnen lieven beminden man inden Heere, ghy hebt eensdeels beproevinge gepasseert, in welcke beproevinge ghy volstandich gebleven zijt, de Heere heb eewigen lof ende prijs van zijnder grooter genaden. Ende ic bidde den Heere daer toe met weenen, dat hy my oock daer toe bequaem maken wil, om zijns naems wille te lijden. [...]

such wonderful promises! I see another beautiful image before my eyes, of a Bride, how she adorns herself to please her Bridegroom of this world. Oh, how then ought we to adorn ourselves, that we might please our Bridegroom! [...] I pray to the Lord night and day, that he will grant us such burning love, so that we do not care what torments they might inflict on us [...]

Know, my dear Husband in the Lord, when I read that you were so very joyful in the Lord, I could not finish the Letter, I had to pray to the Lord that he would grant me, too, the same joy, and keep me to the very end, so that with joy we may present our sacrifice to the glory of our [Mt 6:9] Father who is in heaven, and to the edification of all dear brothers and sisters. [Acts 20:32] With this I want to commend you to the Lord, and the word of his mercy. Know that I thank you very much for your Letter which you wrote me. The grace of the Lord be with us always.

*Another Letter from Lijsken written to her Husband* (excerpts):

[...] I wish us both the crucified Christ as a Protector and Shepherd of our Souls. He himself will keep us in all righteousness, holiness and truth to the very end, and he will also keep us as his sons and daughters, if we keep our [Heb 3:14] Devotion to his being until the very end, indeed, as the [Zech 2:8] apple of his eye. Therefore let us trust in him, and he will not [Heb 13:5] desert us in eternity, but will preserve us as he has done for his own from the beginning of the world. Let us not [1 Cor 10:13] be seized by any temptation except those which are human. The Lord is faithful (says Paul), he will not let us be tested beyond our ability. [2 Cor 1:3] Thanks be to God the Father of our Lord Jesus Christ, who has made us [Acts 5:41] worthy to suffer for his name a short mortal suffering for such beautiful promises that he has made to us, together with all those who remain steadfast in his teaching. [Wis 3:5] In little we may suffer here, but in much will we be rewarded.

My dearly beloved husband in the Lord, you have prevailed through some trials; in those trials you have remained steadfast, the Lord be given eternal praise and glory for his great mercy. And I also pray the Lord, with weeping, that he will make me, too, fitting for that, to suffer for his name's sake [...]

*Een liedeken van Jeronimus Segersz ende zijn Huysvrou Lijsken*

Na de wijse: O Sion wilt u vergaren

Melody after Hortulus cytharae 1582, fol.96v

1   God de Heere is ghetrouwe
    Hy troost de zijne vroech en spaey        2.Cor.1.a.4.
    Als Jeroen met zijn Huysvrouwe
    Leden veel verdriets van die quaey
    So en zijn syniet verlaten        Josue.1.a.5., Hebr.13.a.5.
    Van Godt, in haer druckich tempeest
    Die haer ter noot quam te baten        Ps.91.b.15.
    Seer wonderlijck door zijnen geest.

104

*A Song about Jeronimus Segersz and his Wife Lijsken*

To the Tune: "O Zion wilt thou gather"

1     Most faithful is the Lord our God
       Comforts his own from morn to night.      2 Cor 1:4
       When Jeroen, together with his Wife,
       From evil suffered sorrow great,
       So they were not forsaken      Jos 1:5, Heb 13:5
       By God, in their sad, dark affliction,
       Who in their need did come to aid them,      Ps 91:15
       Through his spirit most wondrously.

2     De Marcgraef met zijn Sophisten
       Quamen met haer craem seer schoon voor
       Maer Jeroen sprack sonder listen:
       Al stont rechtevoort op de door
       En seydt: Ghy muecht wel gaen strijcken
       Segt maer alleen: Het is my leet,
       Ick soude niet willen wijcken
       Want ick heb de waerheyt, ick weet.

3     Doen sprack hy al met verstooren         Marcgraef
       Ick sal u stellen inden vier
       Levendich, wilt ghy niet hooren
       Jeroen belacchende tghetier
       Sprack moedich: Ick wil geern lijden     Acto.21.c.13.
       Al wat ghy my sout moghen doen
       Mijns geloofs halven, (tot strijden
       Was wel gherust die Campioen.)

4     Hy heeft eens twee Papen tsamen
       So gestraft met des Heeren woort
       Dat sy haer wel mochten schamen
       Dies waren sy gram en verstoort
       Dat sy op Jeroen verhetten
       Slaende met vuysten op den Disch
       Seyden dat Petrus insetten
       Tpausdom, Andries dee deerste Mis.

5     Dese ghingen heen ten fijne
       Maer Jeronimus quam ter banck
       Daer hy leet veel smert en pijne
       Gileyns knape rechte hem lanck
       Dus leggende vast gebonden
       Gileyn hem tlijf vol waters goot
       Die wree Wolven om hem stonden
       Verwachtende spraecke ter noot.

6     Als hy alsulcx had gheleden
       Ligghende tusschen mueren vast
       Doen was hy so wel te vreden
       Van hem is ghestreecken den last
       Want hy conde nau gheslapen
       Van grooter blijschap ende vruecht

2   The Markgrave and his fellow Sophists,
    Put on a good show with their wares,
    But Jerome spoke, with no dissembling,
    "And should the fool stand up right now,
    And say: 'The power to leave is in your hands,
    All you need say is: "I regret it"':
    From my course I would not want to stray,
    For I possess the truth, I know."

3   Then he spoke with fury wild:                    Markgrave
    "I'll have you thrown into the fire
    Alive, if you won't hear!"
    Jeroen laughed at all the ranting,
    Spake bravely: "I'll gladly suffer all            Acts 21:13
    Of what you might do unto me,
    For this my faith!" (For doing battle
    Well armed that Champion was).

4   Two Priests he once took on, together,
    Punished them so, with God's own word,
    That they ought well to've been ashamed;
    For that they were angry and enraged,
    They burned with fury at Jeroen,
    Smashing their fists upon the table,
    Insisting that Peter had begun
    The papacy, the first mass held by Andrew.

5   Well, these finally quit the field,
    But Jeronimus to the rack was brought,
    Much he suffered pain and torment,
    Gileyn's helper racked him long,
    And while he lay there, bound up tight,
    With water Gileyn poured him full;
    The cruel Wolves about him stood,
    Expecting his need to make him speak.

6   When he had suffered all of this,
    And lay in strong walls imprisoned,
    He was indeed so much at peace,
    All his burden up and left him,
    For he could hardly get to sleep
    Through rejoicing and joy so great,

Die hy in sKeysers stoel mocht rapen
Vanden Heere hem toeghevuecht.

7   Dus was tSchaep den Wolf ontcomen
    Maer hy ginck Lijsken aen subtijl
    Meynende die vrou tontvromen
    Maer t Godlijck woort was haren stijl.
    En sy is staende ghebleven                      Mat.24.a.13.,
                                                    Mar.13.b.13.
    Teghen des Antichristen hoop
    Die haer hart hebben ghedreven
    Nemende ooc tot de Schrift een loop.

8   Wat wilt ghy Schriftuer useren?                 Paep.
    Gaet henen, en naeyt uwen naet
    Die Apostolen des Heeren
    Wilt ghy navolghen in der daet.
    (Soot schijnt) maer waer is u Tale
    Die spraken door den gheest ghelijck            Acto.2.a.4.
    Seer vyerichlijck altemale
    Met tongen Gods woort autentijck.

9   Maer alle die ghedoopt waren                    Act.2.e.41.
    Van dApostolen, en spraken niet
    Al met tongen voor de scharen
    Het is genoech, na Schrifts bediet
    Dat wy in Christum gelooven
    Die ons beval de Schriftuer pleen               Joan.5.d.39.
    Tondersoecken, die hy bracht van boven
    Want tbest voorsien had Magdaleen.              Luc.10.d.42.

10  Wy lieden zijn die Ghesonden                    Paep.
    Sittende in Moyses Stee
    So comen, na Schrifts vermonden                 Lijsken.
    U toe alle de Ween mee                          Mat.23.
    Daer van wy in Matheo lesen
    Is hy dan ghesonden van Godt                    Paep.
    Die u dus heeft onderwesen?
    Jae, dat weet ick ghewis voor tslot.            Lijsken.

11  Sophisten en Ypocrijten
    Heeftet verdrooten al te seer

7    Thus did the Sheep the Wolf escape;
     But then he turned his craft on Lijsken,
     Thinking he'd make that woman recant;
     But her pillar was the word of God,
     And she endured, remained fast standing      Mt 24:13,
                                                  Mk 13:13
     Against the Antichrist's rough rabble,
     Who so harshly did pursue her,
     Even coming around to Scripture.

8    "And you, you think to use the Scriptures?   Priest
     Go on, be gone, sew your own seam.
     The Lord's Apostles (so it seems)
     You seek to follow in their deeds,
     But where is then your Tongue?
     For right off they spoke through the Spirit,  Acts 2:4
     With greatest passion, altogether,
     God's authentic word, in tongues."

9    "Ah, but all those who were baptized         Acts 2:41
     By the Apostles, they did not
     Speak in tongues, before the crowds.
     It is enough, as Scripture says,
     That in Christ we do believe,
     Who commanded us to search and study         Jn 5:39
     The Scriptures plain brought from above;
     For Mary had chosen the best part."          Lk 10:42

10   "We people here, we have been Sent,          Priest
     And Moses do we represent!"
     "Then you, as Scripture does report,         Lijsken
     Will earn all woe and affliction,            Mt 23
     As in Matthew's gospel we do read."
     "And has he then been sent by God,           Priest
     The one who you all this has taught?"
     "Indeed, I know that surely and most finally." Lijsken

11   The Sophists and the Hypocrites,
     So very much were angered,

(Opening lines above stanza 7:)
     Which he gleaned while in the Emperor's chair,
     Granted to him by the Lord.

Dat sy niet mochten verbijten  
Gods kinders, door haer valsche leer  
Aldus is den Raet ghesloten  
Datmen die lieve Schapen soet  
Ter doot henen soude stooten  
So blusten sy haer wreedt gemoet.

12    Jeroen ter offerhant gaende  
Was tot sterven seer wel bereyt  
Grooten Henrick daer oock staende  
Heeft mee lijdtsaem den doot verbeyt  
Sy traden beyde te gader  
Dus totten palen onbevreest  
Verlangende na haren Vader  
Dien sy bevalen haren Gheest.   Psa.31.a.6., Luc.23.e.45.,  
Act.7.g.59.

13    Jeroen moeste zijn beminde  
Laten, dat was hem groot verdriet  
Want sy was bevrucht met kinde  
En als haer baring was geschiet  
Met tormente en arbeyden  
So worpen sy tSchaep in de Schelt  
Neemt voorbeelt om te verbreyden  
Tlof Gods, broeders zijnde gequelt.

That they could not tear to bits
God's children through their teachings false.
And so the Council did decide
That those dear lambs so sweet they would
Cast out, away, to their deaths.
That's how they quenched their cruel hearts!

12  Jeroen, going to the sacrifice,
Was very well prepared to die;
Big Hendrik, standing there as well,
Patiently waited for death with him.
They stepped together, the two of them,
Thus to the stake, and had no fear,
For their Father they did long,
To whom they did commend their Spirit.   Ps 31:6,
                                          Lk 23:46, Acts 7:59

13  Jeroen had to leave his love,
That was for him a sorrow great;
For she was fruitful with their child.
And when she had borne that child,
In torment, with great labour,
They threw that small sheep in the Scheldt.
Take this example to further spread
God's praise to all tormented Brethren.

# ELISABETH van LEEUWARDEN

*Vonnis tegen Lysbet Dircxdochter, 27 mei 1549[1]*

Alsoe Lysbet Dircxdochter teghenwoerdige gevangen voor den hove van Vrieslandt buyten banden van ijsere bekent heeft herdoept te wesen, in diversche conventiclen geweest te zijn, quaet gevoelen gehadt te hebben van den weerdighen heylighen sacremente, dinsettingen der heyligher kercken ende andere articlen tegens onsen heylighen christengeloove, al contrarie die placcaeten van Keye. Mat., ter cause van welcke huere dwalinghen ende ereuren zij bij den procureur generael gevangen es geweest die ... recht begeert ende justicie versocht heeft hem gedaen te worden, contenderende dat die voorscreven gevanghen aen haer lijff gestrafft soude worden ... waertegens de gevangene gehoert zijnde heeft versocht gracie ende genade ... tvoorscreven hoff gesien die confessie van de voornoemte gevangene mitsgaders huere belijdinge ende wederropinghe van heure voorscreven erreuren ende dwalinghen ... condempneert dieselve gevangene bij den watere geexecuteert ende van levene lijve ter doot gebracht te worden. Aldus gepronunchieert ende uuytgesproecken tot Leeuwarden opten blockhuyse den XXVIIen van meye XV[c] negenenveertich.

---

[1] Text: Rijksarchief in Friesland, Criminele Sententiën van het Hof van Friesland, II 1 and 2 (largely unpaginated), rpt. Mellink, *Documenta*, 85.

# ELISABETH van LEEUWARDEN
(drowned May 27, 1549 in Leeuwarden)

*Verdict against Lysbet Dircxdochter, May 27, 1549:*

Since Lysbet Dircxdochter, currently imprisoned, has confessed before the court of Friesland (freely, without iron bonds) that she was rebaptized, has been in various conventicles, has had wrong beliefs about the venerable holy sacraments, the ordinances of the holy church and other articles against our holy Christian faith, all contrary to the decrees of his Imperial Majesty, and because of her heresies and errors has been captured by the procurer general who demands right and justice be done, contending that the aforementioned prisoner should be corporally punished; and whereas the prisoner, having been examined, has asked for grace and mercy ... the aforementioned court, considering the admission of the aforementioned prisoner together with her confession and the recantation of her aforementioned errors and heresies, condemns this same prisoner to be executed by drowning and to be brought from the living body to death. Thus pronounced and spoken at Leeuwarden in the prison[1] the 27th of May, 1549.

---

[1] "blockhuyse", literally "house with a block": in Dutch, "block" refers to a tool in which the legs of prisoners were locked, while in English the "block" was used for beheading. The English "blockhouse" means "fortification" rather than "prison."

## Een Liedeken van Elisabeth

Na de wijse vanden tweeden Psalm, Ofte:
Roosken root seer wijt ontloken.

Melody: Souterliedeken 2

1 Twas een maechdeken van teder leden
Elisabeth dat was haren naem
De welcke was woonachtich ter steden
Van Leeuwerden een Stede bequaem.

2 In Januario wert sy gevangen,
Het was int vijftienhonderste Jaer
Negenenveertich, sy had verlangen
Nae Christum, dien sij beleet aldaer.     Mat.10.d.32.

3 Men brachtse opt Blockhuys in corter wijle
Daer hebben sy haer ghedrongen an
By haer eedt te seggen, na sWets stijle
Ofte sy niet hadde eenen Man.

## *A Song of Elisabeth*

To the tune of the second Psalm or:
"Rose so red in fullest bloom"

1      There was a maid of tender limbs,
       Elisabeth was her name,
       Who was within a city dwelling,
       The lovely city of Leeuwarden.

2      She was imprisoned in January,
       In the fifteen hundredth year
       And forty-nine; she was longing
       For Christ, whom she professed to there.     Mt 10:32

3      She was brought to prison in short order,
       There they pressed her from all sides,
       To tell under oath, as was law's custom,
       Whether she wasn't married to a man.

| | | |
|---|---|---|
| 4 | Sij heeft geantwoort, als sy dit hoorden<br>Te sweeren ons geensins betaemt<br>Ja ja, neen neen, sullen zijn ons woorden<br>Ick en ben met geenen man versaemt. | |
| 5 | Men seyt als dat ghy verleyt veel lieden<br>En dat ghy ooc een leeraersse zijt<br>Dus wilmen dat ghy sult bedieden<br>Wie ghy geleert hebt in u tijt. | Den Raet. |
| 6 | Och neen mijn Heeren laet my met vreden<br>Van desen, en vraecht na mijn geloof<br>Geern wil ick u daer van geven reden<br>Heeft sy gesproocken voor blint en doof. | Elisabeth. |
| 7 | Mer wat ist dat ghy hout van die misse<br>Ende dat hoochweerdige sacrament<br>Van sulcx en las ick noyt yet gewisse<br>Mer wel van sheeren Avontmael jent. | Den Raet.<br><br>Elisabeth.<br>Mat.26.b.25.,<br>1.Cor.11.c.22. |
| 8 | Sy sprac so veel schrifts ter selver stonde<br>Dat sy aldaer seyden int gerecht<br>De Duyvel die spreect uut uwen monde<br>Ja niet meer dan zijn Heer is de knecht. | Elisabeth.<br>Joan.13.b.16. |
| 9 | Segt den kinderdoop mach die niet vromen<br>Dat ghy u wederom doopen liet<br>Neen, niet weer ben ick daer toe gecomen<br>Alst eens op mijn geloof was geschiet. | Den Raet.<br><br>Elisabeth.<br>Mar 16.b.15. |
| 10 | Mogen die Priesters oock sondt vergeven<br>Neen sy, hoe soud ick gelooven soo<br>Christus, deenige Priester verheven<br>Die alleen reynicht ons van sonden snoo. | Den Raet.<br>Elisabeth.<br>Heb.7.c.24., Joan.2.a.1. |
| 11 | Daer na sonder lange te verbeyden<br>Brachten sy Lijsbet weer voor den Raet<br>En mits dien lieten sy haer doen leyden<br>In den pijnkelder voor den Hencker quaet. | |

| | | |
|---|---|---|
| 4 | She answered, when she heard this:<br>"To swear behooves us in no way.<br>Our 'yea' shall be 'yea,' and our 'nay,' 'nay':<br>I am not joined to any man." | |
| 5 | "They say you mislead many people<br>And that you are a teacher, too:<br>And so we want that you should tell us<br>Whom in your time you have taught." | Councillor |
| 6 | "Oh no, my Lords, leave me in peace<br>About this; question me about my faith,<br>Gladly will I give you an account of that!"<br>Thus spake she to these blind and deaf. | Elisabeth |
| 7 | "And what do you hold of the mass<br>And of the most holy sacrament?"<br>"Of those I've never read anything certain<br>But I did of the Lord's Supper so fine." | Councillor<br><br>Elisabeth<br>Mt 26:26,<br>1 Cor 11:23 |
| 8 | In that hour she quoted so much Scripture<br>That there in the court they said:<br>"The Devil speaks through your mouth."<br>"Yes, not greater than his Lord is the servant." | <br><br><br>Elisabeth<br>Jn 13:16 |
| 9 | "Pray tell: infant baptism, was it of no avail,<br>Since you had yourself baptized again?"<br>"No, not 'again' did I come to that,<br>For only once was it done through my faith." | Councillor<br><br>Elisabeth<br>Mk 16:16 |
| 10 | "Can Priests also forgive sins?"<br>"Not they, how could I believe that?<br>For Christ is the only Priest exalted,   Heb 7:24, 1 Jn 2:1<br>He alone purifies us of our base sins." | Councillor<br>Elisabeth |
| 11 | Thereafter, without long delay, they brought<br>Elisabeth before the Council again.<br>And with that they had her led<br>Into the torture chamber, before the evil Hangman. | |

| | | |
|---|---|---|
| 12 | Wy hebben u noch alleen tot huyden<br>Niet dan met goedicheyt aengegaen<br>Mer wilt ghy ons vraghen niet beduyden<br>Met hardicheyt willen wy bestaen. | Den Raet. |
| 13 | Sy lieten haer twee duym ijsers setten<br>Als sy niet wilde lijden in lanck<br>So dat sy duym en vingeren pletten<br>Datter tbloet ter nagelen uut spranck. | |
| 14 | Och ick en macht niet langer verdragen,<br>Belijdt, men sal verlichten u pijn<br>Helpt my o Heere, sprac sy met clagen<br><br>Want ghy zijt eenen noothelper fijn. | Elisabeth.<br>Den Raet.<br>Elisabeth<br>Judit.9.a.3. |
| 15 | Belijdt, belijdt, riepen sy ter zijden<br>So salmen u doen verlichten wel<br>Want wy seggen u van te belijden<br>En niet van te roepen tot God snel. | |
| 16 | Maer sy hielt al aen tot God seer vuerich<br>Die haer verlichte, en sy sprac coel<br><br>Wilt my nu vry voort vragen geduerich<br>Want ick als voren geen pijn en voel. | Esa.43.a.2.,<br>1.Co.10.b.13. |
| 17 | Noch twee scroeven setten si op haer schenen<br>Beschaemt my niet, heeft sy doen geseyt<br>Want van eenich mannen my noch genen<br>Sijn hant aen mijn bloot lijf heeft geleyt. | |
| 18 | Mits dien beswijmde sy onder de handen<br>Datmen seyde sy is doot by geval<br>Mer sy ontwect zijnde in de banden<br>Sprac, ic ben niet doot maer leef noch al. | |
| 19 | En wilt ghi dat noch niet spreecken tegen<br>Het welc ghy voor ons bekent hebt hier<br>Neen ick, sprac sy tot haer onverslegen<br>Mer wilt met mijn doot besegelen fier. | Den Raet.<br><br>Elisabeth.<br>Apo.2.b.10. |

| | | |
|---|---|---|
| 12 | "Until today we have approached you<br>With nothing except kindness.<br>But should you refuse answer to our questions,<br>We will continue with harshness!" | Councillor |
| 13 | They had two thumbscrews put on<br>When for a long time she refused to confess,<br>So that they smashed thumb and fingers<br>Till the blood spurted out from her nails. | |
| 14 | "Oh, I can bear it no longer!"<br>"Confess, and we will ease your pain!"<br>"Help me, oh Lord!" she spoke, lamenting,<br><br>"For you are a helper in need so fine." | Elisabeth<br>Councillor<br>Elisabeth<br>Jdt 9:4 |
| 15 | "Confess, confess!" they urged from all sides,<br>"Then your pain will be made to ease,<br>For we are telling you of confession<br>And not of calling on God so quick!" | |
| 16 | But with fire she kept on calling to God,<br>Who eased her pain, and she spoke calmly:<br><br>"Go ahead, feel free to continue the questions,<br>For as before I no longer feel pain." | Is 43:2,<br>1 Cor 10:13 |
| 17 | They set two more screws on her shins.<br>"Do not disgrace me," she then said,<br>"For of all men there is not yet one<br>Has laid his hand on my naked body." | |
| 18 | With that she fainted under their hands<br>So that they said, "She has died by accident."<br>But she, awaking, still in bonds,<br>Said: "I am not dead, but I'm quite alive." | |
| 19 | "And will you still not speak against that<br>Which to us here you've confessed?"<br>"Not I," she said to them, undaunted,<br>"But I want to seal it proudly with my death." | Councillor<br><br>Elisabeth<br>Rev 2:10 |

20    In Martio in den Jare voorsproocken
       Gaf over haer een oordeel den Raet
       Met drencken hebben sy haer ghewroken
       Aen dat lief Schaepken, die Wolven quaet.

21    Och laet ons aenmercken metter herten
       Elisabeths mannelijck gemoet
       Wanneer sy ter noot leet pijn en smerten
       Heeft aengeroepen den Heere goet.    Psal.3.a.5., 120.a.1.

       FINIS.

20  In March of the year just mentioned,
    The Council pronounced its judgement on her.
    With drowning they took their revenge
    On this dear lamb, those evil Wolves!

21  Ach, in our hearts let us make note of
    Elisabeth's manly courage,
    How she, in need, bore pain and sorrow
    And called upon the Lord so good.                Ps 3:5, 120:1

## MARY van BECKOM and URSEL van WERDUM

Na de wijse: De Mey staet nu in zijnen tijt.

Droef-heyt wil ick nu laten staen
En sin-gen met ver-blij - - - den
Van Ma-ry van Bec-kom hef ick aen
Die om Gods woort moest lij - - - den.
Haer moe-der dreef-se ten huy-se uut
Het quam int sticht van U-trecht o-ver-luyt
Den Stadt-hou-der ginck-ment ver-mon - den
Dus heeft hy na haer ge-son - - - den.

*Melody: Souterliedeken 73*

## MARY van BECKOM and URSEL van WERDUM
### (burned November 13, 1544 in Delden)

To the tune: "The May is at the height of bloom."

1    Sorrow will I put behind me
And sing with heartfelt joy:
Mary of Beckom's tale I'll begin:
She had to suffer for God's word.
Her mother drove her from their home;
This tale became known in the diocese of Utrecht;
It was reported to the Governor,
And therefore he summoned her to him.

**V**an twe Joffrouwen van Beckom, genaemt Mari ende Ursel, te Delden verbrandt, Int Jaer. 1544. in November.

Na de wijse: De Mey staet nu in zijnen tijt.

1 Droefheyt wil ick nu laten staen
En singen met verblijden
Van Mary van Beckom hef ick aen
Die om Gods woort moest lijden
Haer moeder dreefse ten huyse uut
Het quam int sticht van Utrecht overluyt
Den Stadthouder ginckment vermonden
Dus heeft hy na haer gesonden.

2 Gosen van Raesvelt quam gedraeft
Om dees Jonckvrouwe te vangen
Met veel mannen gestoct gestaeft        Mat.26.e.46.
En grooten prael behangen
Op Beckoms huys daer Mary was
Sy moest opstaen vant bedde seer ras
En met Raesvelt heen trecken
Sy was bereyt sonder schrecken.        Act.21.b.13.

3 Sy siende daer menich man subijt
Sprack aen haer broeders vrouwe
Wilt ghy mede reysen nu ter tijt
En my geselschap houwen
Ursel daer op antwoorde vry
Ick wil geern trecken met dy
Wil Jan van Beckom dat lijden
Wy willen in den Heere verblijden.        Phil.4.a.4.

4 Als Mary dat van haer broeder begeert
Gaf hy consent in desen
Dus heeft Ursel die vrouwe weert
Trou aen haer suster bewesen

f two noblewomen of Beckom named Mary and Ursel, burned in Delden in the year 1544, in November.

To the tune: "The May is at the height of bloom"

1  Sorrow will I put behind me
   And sing with heartfelt joy:
   Mary of Beckom's tale I'll begin:
   She had to suffer for God's word.
   Her mother drove her from their home;
   This tale became known in the diocese of Utrecht[1];
   It was reported to the Governor,
   And therefore he summoned her to him.

2  Gosen van Raesvelt[2] came a-trotting
   To capture this noble maid,
   And many men with sticks and staves,         Mt 26:47
   Decked out in greatest finery.
   Mary was living at the Beckom estate;
   She was rousted from her bed most hastily
   To travel away with Raesvelt:
   But she was prepared and without fear.       Acts 21:13

3  Unexpectedly seeing there so many men,
   Mary turned to her brother's wife:
   "Would you travel with me in this hour
   And keep me company?"
   To which on her own accord Ursel replied:
   "I will gladly travel with you
   If Jan van Beckom will suffer it;
   We will rejoice in the Lord."                Phil 4:4

4  When Mary asked this of her brother,
   He granted her request.
   Thus that worthy woman, Ursel,
   Her troth to her sister proved.

---

[1] "Het sticht van Utrecht" refers to the "Bishopric of Utrecht"; its jurisdiction included the area of Overijssel, where Beckom, the estate of Mary's family, was located, as well as the city of Deventer where the trial was held.

[2] Goesen van Raesveld was the arresting sheriff, but also a blood relative who stood to gain by her death: see the discussion of these two women in the introduction.

Hier was de liefde int herte groot
Stercker dan die bitter doot Cant.8.a.6.
Ja vaster dan die Helle
O lieffelijck versellen.

5 Haer moeder tot haer gecomen was
Uut Vrieslant seer verre gelegen
Met hare susters op dat pas
Dit en mocht haer niet bewegen
Sy heeft genomen haer afscheyt
Van haer moeder sonder verbeyt
Sy vercoos ongemack te lijden Heb.11.c.25.
En tooch met haer suster ten strijde.

6 Sy zijn gevoert na Deventer waert
Voor de blinde Sophisten
Smenschen geset na haerder aert
Brachten sy voort met listen
Wy houden aen Gods woort met vliet
Op sPaus geset achten wy niet
Want daer door (sonder falen)
Die gantsche werelt dwalen.

7 Broer grouwel is ooc gehaelt daer by
Hy wildese vele leeren
Maer na tbetaem en conde hy
Tzijn niet schriftelijck beweeren
Doen hyse niet overwinnen en cont
De Duyvel spreect uut uwen mont Joan.8.e.48.
Sprack hy ter selver ure
Heen wech, heen wech na den vuyre.

8 Sy hebben haer hoochlijck verblijt Act.5.e.42.
Dat sy weerdich waren bevonden
Te lijden met Christo gebenedijt
Sy loofden Godt ten dien stonden
Seggende: Nu is ons geschiet
Dat sy van Christo hebben bediet
Hy moest een inhebber wesen
Des duyvels, so wy lesen. Joan.8.e.48.

|   |   |   |
|---|---|---|
|   | For there was great love in their hearts, |   |
|   | Stronger than that bitter death, | S of S 8:6 |
|   | Yea, mightier than any Hell, |   |
|   | Oh, what sweet union! |   |
| 5 | Ursel's mother had come to her |   |
|   | From Friesland, which so distant lay, |   |
|   | With her sisters, especially for this occasion; |   |
|   | Still, this had no effect on her. |   |
|   | She bad adieu, took her leave |   |
|   | From her mother, without delay. |   |
|   | She chose to endure great hardship | Heb 11:25 |
|   | And marched with her sister into battle. |   |
| 6 | Over to Deventer they were brought, |   |
|   | Before those Sophists blind; |   |
|   | The laws of men, such tricky ruses, |   |
|   | They trotted out most deftly. |   |
|   | "With zeal to God's word we hold fast, |   |
|   | And pay no heed to the Pope's decree; |   |
|   | For through it (without a doubt) |   |
|   | The whole world has gone astray." |   |
| 7 | Brother Grouwel[3], too, was called upon, |   |
|   | He sought to teach them much; |   |
|   | But he was unable, in civil fashion, |   |
|   | To prove his point from Scripture. |   |
|   | And when he couldn't vanquish them: |   |
|   | "The Devil speaks out of your mouth!" | Jn 8:48 |
|   | He said, in that same hour, |   |
|   | "Away with you! away to the pyre!" |   |
| 8 | They were greatly filled with joy | Acts 5:41 |
|   | That they had been found worthy |   |
|   | To suffer with Christ, blessed be he. |   |
|   | They praised God in that hour, |   |
|   | Saying: "Now does befall us |   |
|   | What they have told of Christ, |   |
|   | That he must have been possessed | Jn 8:48 |
|   | By the Devil, as we read." |   |

---

[3] Bernard Grouwell, or Gruwel, was prior of the Dominican friary in Zwolle, a city in Overijssel close to Deventer (Cramer, *Het Offer*, 511).

9   Daer na brachtmense op dat huys
    Te Delden hooge van mueren
    Om af te trecken met confuys
    Bedreven sy veel cueren
    Dies hadden sy seer cleynen lof
    Sy dedent uut tBorgoensche Hof
    Een Commissarius daer comen
    Om die vrouwen te ontvromen.

10  Doen hy gecomen was daer by
    Dede hy voort seer schoone
    Maer dopgeproncte cremery
    Mocht gelden niet een boone
    Van Missen was zijn fondament
    Des Paus statuyten sonder ent
    Daer mede cond hy niet halen
    Tegens de Schrift, hy moeste falen.

11  Voort heeft hy haer gevraget snel
    Oft sy wederdoopers weeren
    Neen seyden sy, wy zijn eens wel
    Gedoopt na Christus leeren
    Want den geloovigen de Heer                Mat.16.c.16.
    Dat bevolen heeft na en veer
    So deden dApostelen hier op aerden    Act.2.c.41., 8.d.37.
    Na tbevel Christi van waerden.

12  Daer mach maer zijn een doope recht        Eph.4.a.5.
    Als de schrift ons tuycht seer schoone
    So wie hier mede is beweecht
    Heeft aengedaen Christum ydoone            Gala.3.c.27.
    Onstraffelijck in leven en leer
    Door den heyligen Geest van den Heer
    Dits haer consciency een vast verbonde     1.Pet.3.c.21.
    Waer door sy staen op Christus gronde.

13  Hy vraechde oft sy int Sacrament
    Oock eten Godt geheele
    Hoe moecht ghy vragen doch so blent
    Vant avontmael houden wy vele              Mat.26.c.25.
    God en wil hebben geen gelijck             Exo.20.a.4.
    Op aerden noch in hemelrijck

9   Thereupon to the fortress they were brought
    In Delden, with its walls so high;
    To destroy their faith, the others
    —to their disgrace!—
    performed a lot of tricks.
    From the Burgundian court they summoned
    A Commissioner to come to them,
    To cause these women to weaken.

10  When he arrived on the scene
    He feigned a sweet demeanour,
    But that dazzling array of fancy wares
    Didn't amount to a hill of beans.
    His faith's foundation was the Mass,
    And Papal decrees, ad nauseam:
    With those beliefs he could not win
    Against Scripture: he was doomed to fail.

11  Further he asked them, sharply,
    If they were Anabaptists.
    "No," they replied, "we have been baptized properly
    Just the once, according to Christ's teachings.
    For the Lord commanded his believers                Mk 16:16
    Precisely that, far and wide
    Thus also did the Apostles here on earth    Acts 2:41, 8:37
    According to our worthy Christ's command."

12  "There is to be only one true baptism,               Eph 4:5
    As Scripture testifies to us so wonderfully,
    And whoever is moved by this
    Has put on Christ so beautiful,                     Gal 3:27
    Unblemished, pure in life and teaching
    Through the Holy Spirit of the Lord.
    This is a firm covenant for their conscience       1 Pet 3:21
    Through which they stand on Christ's foundation."

13  He also asked whether, in the Sacraments,
    They eat God, completely.
    "How can you ask so blindly?
    We revere the Lord's Supper;                        Mt 26:26
    But God will suffer no likeness of him               Ex 20:4
    On earth nor in heaven.

      Ick bent, ick bent, anders geen meere    Esa.43.b.11., 46.a.8.
      Spreeckt hy door des Propheten leere.

14    Oock vinden wy beschreven fijn
      Hoe Christus heeft nagelaten
      Tot gedenck zijns doots, broot ende wijn
      Dat hy gaf zijn vleys tot onser baten
      So vaeck wy willen breken dit broot    1.Cor.11.c.25.
      Sullen wy spreken van zijnen doot
      So ons tuycht Paulus leere
      Tot dat coemt Christus de Heere.

15    Als sy nu hielden voor kettery
      Al dat Paus oyt in stelden
      So is derthiene Novembri
      Die Banck gespannen tot Delden
      Mary en Ursel quamen saen
      Voor Pilato en Caypha staen
      Daer sy ter doot werden verwesen
      Maer sy verblijden haer in desen.

16    Nu geschiet ons na Christus leer
      Dat die Discipel niet te boven    Mat.10.c.24., Joan.13.b.16.
      Gaet zijn Meester, oft knecht de Heer
      Dus gingen sy Godt loven
      Alst volck haer bestandicheyt sach aen
      Storten sy so menigen traen
      Doenmense voerde na die staken
      Songen sy met vruechden en spraken.

17    Screyt niet om tgeen datmen ons aendoet    Luce.23.c.27.
      Wy lijden niet als toveneeren

   'I am, I am God, there is none like me,'    Is 43:11, 46:9
   He spake through the teaching of the Prophets."

14  "What's more, we find described so fine
   How Christ left us the bread and wine,
   In remembrance of his death,
   And that he gave his body for our salvation;
   As often as we break this bread      1 Cor 11:25
   We do remember his death
   (As Paul's teaching testifies to us)
   Until Christ the Lord comes again."

15  Since they now held as heresy
   All that the Pope had ever decreed,
   So, on the thirteenth of November
   The Court was called at Delden.
   In short order Mary and Ursel came
   To stand before Pilate and Caiaphas[4];
   There they were sentenced to death:
   But they themselves rejoiced at this.

16  "Now it befalls us as Christ has taught,
   That the Disciple is not above      Mt 10:24, Jn 13:16
   His Master, nor the servant above his Lord":
   Thus they began to praise God.
   When the people observed their steadfastness
   They wept many a tear.
   When the women were led to the stakes,
   They sang with joy and spake:

17  "Do not mourn that which is done to us,    Lk 23:27
   For we do not suffer as might witches[5]

---

[4] Pilate was Roman Governor of Judea AD 26-36, Caiaphas the ruling high priest of the Sanhedrin AD 18-36, the highest Jewish court (see commentary to Mark 14:53 - 15:15 in the *NIV Study Bible*). The parallel is clear: just as Jesus was put to death through the combined injustice of secular and religious institutions, so their sixteenth-century secular and religious equivalents unjustly condemned the Anabaptists.

[5] The criminals listed in 1 Pet 4:15 include murderers, thieves, evildoers, busybodies, in contrast to those who suffer as Christians; it would seem that by adding "toveneeren," which can be translated as "magicians" as well as "witches," the poet emphasizes that Anabaptists were being persecuted not for the kind of consorting with the devil of which witches were accused, but for true and legitimate faith in God.

|   | Of ander misdaders, sprac Mari vroet | 1.Pet.4.b.15. |
|---|---|---|
|   | Maer by Christum tzijn is ons begeeren |   |
|   | Gelooft sy Godt dat wy die stont |   |
|   | Beleeft hebben, seyden sy int ront |   |
|   | Bekeert u, blijft op Gods woort staende | Eze.18.d.30. |
|   | So salt u eewich zijn wel gaende. |   |

18     Doen nu die tijt des lijdens quam aen
        Heeft Mari blijdlijck ontloken
        Lieve suster den Hemel is opgedaen
        Als Stephanus heeft gesproken        Acto.7.f.56.
        Dat wy nu lijden in corter tijt              1.Pe.1.a.6.
        Dies sal ons siel eewich zijn verblijt
        En met Christo ons Bruygom leven
        Dus wil ik u de cus des vreeds gheven.     2.Cor.13.b.12.

19     Sy baden God inden hoogen Throen
        Vergheeft haer doch de sonden     Luc.23.c.33., Acto.7.f.66.
        Want sy niet weten wat sy doen
        Noch hoordemen haer vermonden
        De werelt is nu seer doof en blint
        Ontberm dy over dijn dochteren en kint
        En laet ons niet van dy wijcken
        Neemt ons siel in dijn eewich Rijcke.

20     Eerst namen sy Mary, die badt seer soet
        Doverheyt sonder verdrieten
        Dat sy doch dat onschuldich bloet
        Niet meer souden vergieten
        Sy viel op haer knyen ter neer
        En sprack haer gebedt al totten Heer
        Vyerich in haren nooden
        En bad noch voor die haer dooden.        Acto.7.f.60.

21     Daer na spranc sy met vrijen moet
        Op den houte met verblijden
        Ick macht vertellen niet so soet
        Als sy bereyt was te lijden
        Dy Christo heb ick overgegeven my
        En weet, dat ick eewich leven sal met dy
        O Vader in sHemels foreeste     Luc.22.d.46., Acto.7.f.59.
        In u handt beveel ick mijn geeste.

|    | Or other criminals," spake Mary wisely, | 1 Pet 4:15 |
|    | "But our desire is to be with Christ. | |
|    | Praise be to God that we have lived | |
|    | To see this hour," they said to those around them, | |
|    | "Repent, remain steadfast in God's word, | Ezek 18:30 |
|    | And it will go well with you eternally." | |

18    And when the time of suffering drew nigh,
Mary revealed most joyfully:
"Dearest Sister, Heaven has been opened
As Stephen once told;                     Acts 7:56
That we now suffer for a season           1 Pet 1:6
Means that our souls rejoice eternally
And live with Christ our Bridegroom;
Therefore I greet you with the kiss of peace."   2 Cor 13:12

19    They prayed to God Enthroned on high:
"Do forgive them their sins       Lk 23:34, Acts 7:60
For they know not what they do."
And further they could be heard to say:
"The world is now most deaf and blind:
Have mercy on your daughters and children,
And do not let us forsake you,
Take our soul into your eternal Kingdom."

20    First they took Mary, who, without distress,
Most sweetly beseeched the authorities
That they should not spill
Any more of such innocent blood.
She fell down to her knees
And spoke her prayer to the Lord,
Most passionately in her need,
And prayed even for her executioners.         Acts 7:60

21    Thereupon, with spirit free, she sprang
Onto the wood, rejoicing.
Words fail me to tell as sweetly
As she was prepared to suffer.
"To you, O Christ, do I commend myself,
And know that I shall live with you eternally.
O Father, in Heaven's green wood grove,   Lk 23:46, Acts 7:59
Into your hand I commend my spirit."

22  De Hencker vloecte met quaden moet
    Die keten was niet na zijnen sinne
    Och vrient, denct hoe qualijc dat ghy doet
    Sprac sy uut vyeriger minne
    Mijn lichaem en is des weerdich niet
    Dat Christo daer over lastering geschiet
    Betert u leven tot deser stonde     Mat.4.b.17., Mar.1.b.25.
    Dat ghy niet brant in hellen gronde.

23  Die Predicant was daer ontrent
    Die een Leeraer is tot Delden
    Hy heeft Ursel omgewent
    Maer sy keerde haer met gewelde
    Laet my sien deynde myns susters soet
    Sprack sy al uut een dringent gemoet
    Want die heerlijcheyt daer sy sal ganghen
    Begeer ick van herten te ontfangen.

24  Sy quamen haer naerder by cant
    En vraechden met practijcken
    Haer suster was deerlijck verbrant
    Oft sy niet wilde afwijcken
    Neen, om den doot die ghy my aendoet
    Wil ick niet overgeven deewich goet
    Sout ghy my van de waerheyt drijven
    Neen, by Christum wil ick vroom blijven.

25  Men wilde noch eeren Ursel soet
    Brengende tsweert ter handen
    Neen, sprack sy, mijn vleys is niet te goet
    Om Christum te verbranden
    Segt Jan van Beckom goede nacht
    Heeft sy tot een van haer Meyers gesacht
    Dat hy Godt diene sonder vresen     Luc.1.f.69.
    Ick sal Godt een offer wesen.

26  Als Ursel quam den houte ontrent
    Sloech sy hare handen te gare
    Onse Vader die zijt in sHemels tent     Mat.6.b.9.
    Ja, sprac die Paep, daer vintmen voorware
    Dat ick hem daer soeck in desen noot
    Moet ick sterven den tijtlijcken doot

| | | |
|---|---|---|
| 22 | The Deathsman swore with angry heart, | |
| | For there was something wrong with the chains. | |
| | "Ach, friend, think of the wrong you do!" | |
| | She spoke with passionate love. | |
| | "My body is not worth the honour | |
| | That Christ would be blasphemed for it! | |
| | Better your life in this very hour | Mt 4:17, Mk 1:25 |
| | So you won't burn in the depths of hell!" | |
| | | |
| 23 | That Dominican was there on the scene, | |
| | The one who's a Preacher in Delden; | |
| | He sought to turn Ursel away, | |
| | But she resisted him, turning back forcibly. | |
| | "Let me see my sweet sister's end," | |
| | She spoke, with an urgency of spirit, | |
| | "For the glory into which she'll enter | |
| | I long to receive with all my heart." | |
| | | |
| 24 | They pressed her hard from all sides, | |
| | And asked with all the tricks they'd learned: | |
| | Her sister had been miserably burned - | |
| | And wouldn't she renounce her ways? | |
| | "No, never: for the death you can inflict, | |
| | I would not surrender my eternal inheritance; | |
| | Would you drive me from the truth? | |
| | Never. With Christ will I remain undaunted." | |
| | | |
| 25 | Still, they wanted to honour Ursel sweet | |
| | By bringing the sword to hand. | |
| | "No," spoke she, "my flesh is not too precious | |
| | To be burned for Christ. | |
| | Bid Jan van Beckom farewell," | |
| | She said to one of her Stewards. | |
| | "Let him serve God without fear, | Lk 1:74 |
| | I will be a sacrifice to God." | |
| | | |
| 26 | When Ursel came up to the pyre, | |
| | She clasped her hands together. | |
| | "Our Father, who art in the tent of Heaven..." | Mt 6:9 |
| | "Yes," said the Papist, "there you'll find, for sure!" | |
| | "Because I seek him there in this my need, | |
| | I must die this untimely death; | |

Woud ick hem int broot bekennen
Ick mocht mijn leven verlengen.

27  Doen Ursel trat opt houte vry
Ist haer onder die voet ontgleden
My dunct ick valle af, sprack sy
Seer ras hoorde die Tyran de reden
Hy riep, hout, sy afwijcken wil
Neen, dat block ontgaet my sonder geschil
In Gods woort wil ick niet beswijcken
By Christum blijf ick stadelijcken.

28  Dus zijn dese Schaepkens totten ent
Beyde volstandich gebleven                   Mat.10.b.22.
En hebben met haer doot present
Gods woort een zegel gegeven
Sy zijn met grooter lijdtsaemheyt
Door gestreden in vromicheyt
En hebben ons gelaten
Een exempel, wilt dit vaten.

29  O Heer verhoort doch ons geclach
Wilt dese dagen vercorten                    Mt.24.b.22.
En uwen Geest sonder verdrach                Joan.15.c.26.
In onse herten storten
Geeft ons ooc stercheyt in der noot
Aldus te strijden totter doot
Dat wy met groot verlangen
Die croon met haer ontfangen.                4.Esd.2.e.43.

> If I were to confess he's in the bread,
> I could prolong my life."

27 When Ursel stepped freely on the wood,⁶
It slipped away from under her foot.
"I think I'm falling away," she said.
The Tyrant heard her words immediately;
He called: "Halt! she wants to recant!"
"No, the block slips under me, without a doubt,
From God's word I will not depart,
With Christ I will continue faithfully."

28 And so until the bitter end, these Lambs,
Both of them, endured faithful      Mt 10:22
And with their deaths recounted here
Gave to God's word a seal.
With great and patient suffering
They fought to the end with courage brave,
And have left for us
An exemplum—understand this well.

29 O Lord, do hear our crying,
We beseech you, shorten these days,      Mt 24:22
Pour into our hearts
Your Spirit, without delay.      Jn 15:26
Give us strength, too, in our need,
Like them, to battle to the death,
So that with greatest longing
We may receive the crown with them.      2 Esd 2:43

---

⁶ The "wood" is the "block" of line 7 of this stanza, an apparatus used to lock the legs of criminals. In this stanza the poet uses words with double meaning which do not translate well into English: "afvallen"(line 3) is both "to fall off" something, as happens to Ursel with the block of wood, and "to fall away from the faith", which is the Inquisitor's interpretation and why he calls a halt to the execution; a recantation at this late hour would be a tremendous coup for orthodoxy. Of course this does not happen.

# SIX WOMEN OF ANTWERP

*Melody after Hortulus cytharae 1582, fol.96v*

# SIX WOMEN OF ANTWERP

Maayken de Cat, drowned July 29, 1559
Magdalena Andriesdochter, drowned July 29, 1559
Aechtken, Adriaen Jorisdochter, executed (beheaded?) July 29, 1559
Maeyken Sprincen, drowned October 12, 1559
Margriet van Halle, drowned (or beheaded?) October 12, 1559
Maeyken de Corte, executed (beheaded?) October 12, 1559

To the tune: "O Zion, wilt thou gather"

1   The warrants of Babel's Council
    Are executed thus
    By her Servants: such Regents
    Plunder and capture with armed force,
    Betray with many sons of Judas;
    They seek only their own gain,
    Shamefully great, to their own ruin,
    That goods-hungry, blood-thirsty rabble!

**V**an ses vroupersoonen binnen Antwerpen gedoot, vier verdroncken, ende twee onthooft, int Jaer 1559. Soect hare namen int liet van de 72 vrienden.

Na de wijse: O Sion wilt u vergaren.

1 Babels Raets Mandamenten
  Worden aldus volbracht
  Door haer Dienaers, sulcke Regenten
  Rooven, vangen metter macht
  Met veel der Judassen verraden
  Die al soecken haer gewin
  Schandelijck groot tot haerder schaden
  Dat goetgierich, bloetgierich gesin.

2 Doemen schreef duysent vijfhondert
  Ende negenenvijftich Jaer
  Doen hebben dees Roovers geplondert
  Gevangen genomen daer
  Ses geloovige ten fijne
  Van Christus Scholieren jent
  Mijn vruechde moeste verdwijnen
  Doen ickse sach in sulck torment.

3 Den twintichsten dach in Meye
  Quamen de Roovers metter macht

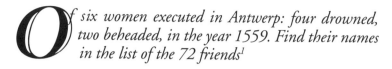

Of six women executed in Antwerp: four drowned, two beheaded, in the year 1559. Find their names in the list of the 72 friends¹

To the Tune: "O Zion, wilt thou gather"

1   The warrants of Babel's Council
    Are executed thus
    By her Servants: such Regents
    Plunder and capture with armed force,
    Betray with many sons of Judas;
    They seek only their own gain,
    Shamefully great, to their own ruin,
    That goods-hungry, blood-thirsty rabble!²

2   It was the year they wrote
    a thousand five hundred and fifty-nine,
    That these Robbers came and plundered
    And took as captives there
    Six believers, the finest
    Of Christ's Pupils so noble;
    All of my joy did have to vanish
    When I saw their great torment.

3   It was on the twentieth day of May
    When the Robbers came with arms and force

---

¹ The 25-stanza "Song of LXXII Friends" (*Offer*, 563-568) lists the names of 72 Anabaptists martyred in Antwerp from 1555 to 1560; it dedicates verse 17, lines 5-8 and verse 18 to the six women commemorated here. The sources provide conflicting information on the manner of execution of these women: according to the "72 friends" song Margriet van Halle and Maeyken de Corte were beheaded, the others drowned; archival records state that Aechtken and Maeyken de Corte were "executed," the others drowned (*Antwerpsch Archievenblad* IX, 9-10); the song translated here states only that four were drowned, two beheaded; according to Braght's *Martelaers-Spiegel* Margriet van Halle and Maeyken de Corte were beheaded, the others drowned (250). Of interest, ultimately, is that the historical record does agree on the basics: these women were executed, four by drowning, two in another manner.

² The language of the last four lines of stanza one is obscure, though the intent is clear enough: a characterization of "the enemies" who persecute the Anabaptists as sons of the arch-betrayer Judas, like him intent on personal gain.

In des Marckgraven Leye
Die hy daer mede heeft gebracht
Om te rooven tot dien stonden
Als verschuerende Wolven wreet
De Schapen die sy vonden
Hebben sy met haer geleet.

4   Stoutmoedich sonder versagen
    Quamen sy gestoct, gestaeft
    Om volbrengen haer aenslagen
    Na den roof quamen sy gedraeft
    En hadden in haerder bende
    Een Judas, tverlooren kint
    Moetwillige dwaelders met blende
    Die al waren eens gesint.

5   Door sVerraders listige lagen
    Hadden sy de huysen bespiet
    Van te voren vele dagen
    Ten laetsten so isset geschiet
    Dat sy de huysen in namen
    Met gewelt tegen recht voorwaer
    Sy mogent haer wel schamen
    Haer fortsich gewelt is openbaer.

6   Dus namen sy tot dien stonden
    Twee huysen in metter spoet
    Ses vrou persoonen sy daer vonden
    Int geloof sterck als mannen gemoet
    Na tvleesch, machmen wel meenen
    Onverhoets waren sy versaecht
    Want vrouwen herten zijn geen steenen
    Daert also stormt en vlaecht.

7   De Roovers cloeck in haer hantieren
    Doorliepen de huysen overal
    Die sy sochten in haer bestieren
    En vonden sy niet, 't was haer misval

Into the Margrave's Avenue.³
Those he brought along with him
To do the plundering in that hour,
Like cruel Wolves devouring prey,
They carted away with them
Those little Sheep which they did find.

4   Intrepidly and without fear
They came full-armed, cudgeled and staved,
To carry out their brave attacks.
For the plunder they came a-running,
And had within their rabbling band
One Judas, that lost child,
Willful wanderers, blinders on,
All now of a unified mind.

5   Through the Traitor's deceitful counsel,
They had spied out, surveyed the houses
Already for many days before.
And finally this is what happened:
They conquered and took those houses
With force - truly this was against the law
And they should be ashamed of themselves!
Their brute force is publicly known.

6   And so in that very same hour,
In short order they overpowered two houses.
Six female persons there they found,
In their faith strong, as men might be,
Though in the flesh, as one might think,
Caught unawares they did feel fear:
For women's hearts aren't made of stone,
When faced by storms and nasty weather.

7   The Robbers, adroit in their action,
Searched nook and cranny of the houses;
They found not those whom they sought
To take into custody - that was a setback!

---

³ "The Margrave's Avenue" was a location outside of Antwerp where confiscated goods (clothing, household items) of the convicted and executed were sold; records indicate that the property of Maeyken Sprincen, Margriete van Halle, and Maeyken de Corte was disposed of there (Génard, *Antwerpsch Archievenblad*, 16-17).

Dies moeste dat haer spijten
Dat so faelgeerde haer opset
Sverraders beste profijten
Die waren daer seere belet.

*Voor den genen die sy sochten,*
*soude de verrader 300 gulden*
*gehat hebben, so verre*
*sy hem gecregen hadden.*

8   De Marckgraaf was onverduldich
    Dat hem faelgeerde zijn opstel
    De gevangenen onschuldich
    Sach hy aen seer wreet en fel
    Heeft verstoort tot haer gesproken
    (Want hy den gesochten niet vont)
    Ick wou dat ghy te Hoboken
    Te samen op der Heyden stont.

9   Sy antwoorden soetelijcken
    De Heer vol genaden vermaert
    Die de zijne zo trouwelijcken
    Als zijnen oochappel bewaert
    Heeft hem tot dese daghen
    Van uwen handen behoet
    Den wil Gods, en welbehaghen
    Over ons geschieden moet.

10  Te Hoboken op de Heye
    Heeft hy de Schapen niet ghesant
    Maer in des Marckgraven Leye
    Nam hy mede al die hy vant
    De reste moeste hy borgen
    Hy en schout haer daer mee niet quijt
    Ist heden niet, so ist morghen
    Alst pas geeft, en metter tijt.

No doubt they were sorely disappointed
That they so failed in their intentions,
For the traitor was greatly hindered
In reaping the greatest profits for his work.
> The traitor would have received
> 300 gulden for the one
> that they sought, had they
> been able to capture him.

8 The Margrave was beside himself,
For he had failed to achieve his aim;
He glared at those innocent prisoners
Most cruelly and fiercely,
And in a rage said to them
(Not having found the one he sought)
"I wish all of you were to be found
Together at Hoboken on the Heath!"[4]

9 They answered most serenely:
"The Lord, known to be so full of grace,
Who keeps his own as faithfully
As the apple of his eye,
Has even to these very days
Protected him from your hands;
The will of God, and his pleasure
Is all that can be done to us."

10 He did not send those little sheep
To Hoboken on the Heath,
But to the Margrave's Avenue
He took all those whom he found;
For the others he had to postpone their capture,
Though he did not acquit them for that,
And if it isn't today, it will be tomorrow,
When that occasion arises, in due course.

---

[4] "Ik verwens u op de Hobokense Heide" ("I curse you to the Hoboken Heath!") was an expletive used in Antwerp into the eighteenth century, at which time the wild heaths of Hoboken began to be cultivated and settled. First mention of Hoboken as an area of ill-repute was made in 1460; it was the refuge of bandits and robbers as well as one of the places where lepers were cared for. Today Hoboken is one of Antwerp's city districts (with thanks to Raymond Corremans of Antwerp for this information!).

11  Tijt en stont, avont en morghen
    Der Princen herten ydel bedacht                Pro.21.a.1.
    Der menschen raden vol sorghen
    Het staet al in Godes macht
    Sonder Gods lijdtsaem gehingen
    Niet een blat vanden boom en daelt
    Na zijn wil laet hy ons verdringhen
    De goede vande boose verdwaelt.

12  De Roovers voerden den roof binnen
    Met de gevangen quamen sy gaen
    Die droegen haer saet gheestich van sinnen
    Saeyende dat met druckich vermaen              Psa.126.a.5.
    God vader van hier boven
    Sal haer inden grooten dach des Oost
    Bereyden onsterffelijcke schoven
    Dies zijn sy verhuecht en ghetroost.

13  Aldus druckich met haestichede
    Quamen sy in stonden cort
    Binnen Antwerpen de stede
    Daer veel onschuldich bloets wordt gestort
    Inden Kercker ginckmense sluyten
    In donckere Putten onclaer
    Daer laghen sy deerlijck in muyten
    In sdrucx tormenten swaer.

14  Dus gheweldich sy verrasten
    Den onschuldighen goedertier
    De Schaerianten seer brasten
    Maeckten blijdelijk goede chier
    Den roof sy aldus deelen
    Dus verstroyt der Pelgrims aertsch goet
    De goetgierighe de Juweelen
    De bloetgierige crijgen tbloet.

15  Al ist dat de vrome verliesen
    Dit tijtelijcke, dies niet te min
    Door tgheloove sy verkiesen
    Dat eewich is tot haer ghewin

11  The moment, the hour, the evening, the morning,
    The vain thoughts in the hearts of kings,          Pr 21:1
    The pond'rings of man weighed down by care:
    All these things are in God's power.
    Without God's permission, or his consent,
    Not one leaf will fall from the tree;
    According to his will he lets us be displaced,
    The good by the errant bad.

12  The Robbers carried home their prey,
    With their captives they came a-riding;
    These carried their seed, God-fearing of mind
    Sowing it with sorrowful admonition.               Ps 126:5
    In that great day of the East
    God our Father up above
    Will prepare for them immortal sheaves,
    And they shall rejoice and be comforted.

13  And so, downcast and with great haste
    Within a few hours they entered
    Into the city of Antwerp,
    Where innocent blood is so liberally shed.
    They proceeded to lock them in prison,
    In dark Dungeons, gloomy, dirty.
    There they lay, miserable in prison,
    In the burdensome torments of anxious dread.

14  By that sort of force they took by surprise
    Those innocent, most noble souls;
    The Sergeants feasted and gluttonized
    And gleefully indulged in good cheer;
    Their ill-gotten gains they divided thus
    (And so are dispersed the Pilgrims's earthly goods):
    The goods-thirsty gain the Jewels,
    The blood-thirsty gain the blood.

15  And though the faithful should lose
    The things of this earth, it is no matter -
    For through the faith they have chosen
    That which is eternal, to their profit;

Godt sal haer nemmermeer beswijcken  
Daer op zijn sy seer wel ghemoet  
Babel mach haer met practijcken  
Niet scheyden van Gods liefde soet.                    Rom.8.e.35.

16  De liefde Gods verwint seer crachtich  
    Daer tgheloof door de liefde werckt                Gala.5.a.6.  
    Tgheloof is Gods gave warachtich                   Eph.2.a.7.  
    Door liefde zijn wy daer in ghesterckt  
    Gods liefde ghestort in onser herten  
    Door den Gheest der waerheyt gesent  
    Die troost den zijnen in smerten  
    Die om gerechticheyt lijdt torment.

17  In lijden, druck en tormenteren  
    Waren dees vrymoedich gesint  
    Men ginck haer examineren  
    Voor de verkeerde Rechters blint  
    Met Pilato haer handen dwaende                     Mat.27.c.24.  
    Meynen haer onschuldich wasschen net  
    Met sKeysers Placcaet haer ontslaende  
    Maer blijven bloetschuldich besmet.

18  Gods eewich lof te vermeeren  
    Spraken van herten onbevreest  
    Wy gelooven het woort des Heeren  
    Een Vader, Soon, en heylige Geest  
    Dees drie zijn een God warachtich                  1.Joan.5.a.7.  
    Van hem comen alle gaven soet                      Jac.1.b.17.  
    Sijne geboden eendrachtich  
    Beleden sy recht ende goet.

19  Sy gingen twee Maechden pijnen  
    Luttel hadden de Tyrannen acht  
    Dat wy alle in smerte verschijnen  
    Door vrouwen voort worden gebracht  
    Van dees natuerlijck experiency  
    Hebben sy geen redelijcheyt geleert  
    Sy maken daer af cleyn mency  
    Dus zijn sy tyrannich verkeert.

|    | God will never forsake them, | |
| :--- | :--- | ---: |
|    | Their good spirits rest on that promise. | |
|    | Despite all her trickery, Babel cannot separate | |
|    | Them from the love of God so sweet. | Rom 8:35 |
| 16 | The love of God gains much in power | |
|    | Where faith does work through love; | Gal 5:6 |
|    | Faith is truly the gift of God, | Eph 2:8 |
|    | And through love we are strengthened in it; | |
|    | God's love, poured into our hearts | |
|    | Sent by the Spirit of truth, | |
|    | Does comfort His own in their sorrow, | |
|    | Those who suffer torment for the sake of justice. | |
| 17 | In suffering, oppression, and torment, | |
|    | These were still joyfully minded. | |
|    | They started to examine them | |
|    | Before those benighted Judges so blind. | |
|    | Washing their hands with Pilate, they imagine | Mt 27:24 |
|    | They can wash themselves to innocence, | |
|    | By the excuse that it's the Emperor's Decree - | |
|    | Still, they stay soiled with innocent blood. | |
| 18 | To increase the eternal praise of God | |
|    | They spake with fearless heart: | |
|    | "We believe the word of the Lord: | |
|    | One Father, Son, and Holy Ghost; | |
|    | These three are verily one God, | 1 Jn 5:7 |
|    | From him comes every perfect gift." | Jas 1:17 |
|    | With one mind, his laws | |
|    | They confessed, right and good. | |
| 19 | They started to torture two of the maidens: | |
|    | Little did those Tyrants consider | |
|    | That we all emerge on this earth in pain, | |
|    | Brought forth through women; | |
|    | From this natural experience | |
|    | They had learned no reasonableness; | |
|    | They attach little importance to this, | |
|    | So inhumanly astray have they gone. | |

20   Godt die wonderlijck ende crachtich
     In zijn swacke leden openbaert
     Door zijn liefde sterckende machtich
     Heeft hy haren mont wel bewaert
     So dat sy in lijdens trueren
     Getroost waren vrijmoedich fijn
     Met God sprongen over de mueren           Psa.18.c.30.
     Niet vreesende eenich gepijn.

21   Inden Mey werden sy gevangen
     Vande Roovers in handen getrost
     Int lijden was haer verlangen
     Vanden vleesche te zijn verlost
     Om te strijden sonder verflouwen
     Haren strijt tot een salich ent            2.Tim.4.a.7.
     Om tgeloove te behouwen
     Te winnen de Croon excellent.                     4.Es.2.f.43.,
                           2.Tim.4.a.8., Apo.2.b.10.

22   Den achthienden Julij clare
     Eerst drie Maechden zedich gemaniert
     Brachtmen in de Vierschare
     Daermen gewelt tegen recht hantiert
     Den elfsten Octobris int verseeren
     Quamen ter Vierschaer drie vrouwen jent
     Een oude vrou tweevoudich in eeren         2.Tim.5.c.17.
     Een Weduwe eerbaer, met een Dochter van Ghent.

23   Sy zijn op twee stonden verwesen
     Van levende lijve ter doot
     Van de Wolven leelijck begresen
     Ist niet een tyrannije groot
     De vier hebben sy verdroncken
     Int water, so men beesten versmoort
     Twee onthooft, dees ses lieve troncken
     Sijn aldus by nachte vermoort.

24   Christus heeft voor alle geleden           1.Pet.2.c.21.
     De zijn tot een exempel waert
     So zijn hem dees na ghetreden
     Haer leven totter doot niet gespaert
     In Christo volstandich sy bleven

20   God, who so wonderfully and mightily
     Reveals himself in his weak vessels,
     Strengthening them powerfully through his love,
     He guided and kept their speech well,
     So that they, in the sorrows of their suffering,
     Were comforted, and perfectly joyous.
     By their God they leapt over the walls,             Ps 18:29
     And feared neither torture nor pain.

21   It was in May that they were captured
     By the Robbers, trussed up in their hands;
     But in their suffering, their only longing
     Was to be released from the flesh,
     Was to fight the good fight,
     Without flagging to finish the course.              2 Tim 4:7
     They longed to keep the good faith,
     To win the Crown of righteousness.                  2 Esd 2:43,
                                                2 Tim 4:8, Rev 2:10

22   On the eighteenth of July, that glorious day,
     They first brought three maidens, chaste and humble,
     Before the Tribunal, into Court,
     Where might rules at the expense of right;
     On the eleventh of October, in pain and sorrow,
     Three noble women appeared before the Court:
     An old woman, worthy of double honor,               1 Tim 5:17
     An honorable Widow, with a Daughter from Ghent.

23   Within two hours they were sentenced,
     From among the living they were sent to death,
     Cruelly mocked by the Wolves–
     Oh, what bitter tyranny!
     Four of them they drowned
     In a tub of water, like they drown animals,
     Two they beheaded: these six dear kinsfolk
     Were thus murdered in the dead of night.

24   Christ has suffered for us all,                     1 Pet 2:21
     Leaving us an example for his own;
     And so these followed in his footsteps,
     Not sparing their lives, even unto death.
     In Christ they remained constant.

Haer namen zijn hier niet geset
Maer staen in slevens Boeck geschreven  Luc.10.c.20.,
Phil.4.a.3., Apo.21.d.27.
By al die leven na sHeeren Wet.

25 Babels tyrannij moecht ghy sporen
Om dat haer Rijcke wort verstoort
Sy hebben met branden, smoren
Veel gedoot om des Heeren woort
Vervolcht, die in vreden God vreesen
Uut tlant gejaecht, om lijf en goet
Gebrocht, gemaect Weduwen en Weesen
Och wrake roept tonschuldich bloet.  Gen.4.b.10.,
4.Es.15.b.10.

[Een Brief van Maeyken de Korte.]

[2.Thess.3.1.] Myn lieve Suster bid voor ons, dat het Woord des Heeren een voortgang hebbe, en vruchtbaer wesen moet, in alle verduldigheyd en heyligheyd hem verbeyden met lijdsaemheydt, [Apoc.22.12.] al komende sal hy komen, en brengen sijn loon met hem, [1.Thess.5.23.] hy is getrouw die 't belooft heeft, die 't ook doen sal, het is wel gelijk ik segge, [Job.7.1.] onse leven is eenen gedurigen strijd op der aerden, weet dat ik redelijk wel gemoed ben, het vleesch is redelijk, de Heere heb lof, [1.Cor.4.13.] wy zijn hier wel een vloek der werelt, [2.Cor.5.2.] en haken altijds t'huys te zijn, [2.Pet.3.13.] en na een timmering niet met handen gemaekt, maer in den Hemel selve, nieuwe Hemelen en nieuwe Aerde verwachten wy na sijne beloften, waer in de rechtveerdigheyt woont. Hoe sullen wy moeten geschikt wesen met een Godsalig wesen: Ik vinde my dikwils geslagen: ik vinde ook soo veel gebreeken in my, en noch soo veel te sterven, en moet al den Heere met een ootmoedig hert, en beevende verslagen gemoed opgeven, en bidden hem om genade, en niet om recht. Ik gevoele hoe ik my minder make, [1.Cor.1.27., Phil.2.12.] hoe de krachtige God meer in my werkt, en sijn genade meer in my stort: dan weene ik seer bitterlijk, en valle op mijn knyen, en danke mijnen God, en segge: O mijn Heere en God, wat ben ik Adams kindt, dat gy doch sijner gedenkt, gy hebt hem heerlijkheyd gegeven over alle u werken verheven, hoe komt dat gy ons soo rijkelijk besoekt,

Their names are not written here,
But have been recorded in the Book of Life,    Lk 10:20,
Phil 4:3, Rev 21:27
With all who live by the law of the Lord.

25    You feel the weight of Babel's tyranny
Because her kingdom is disrupted, threatened;
With burning, with drowning,
They have killed many for the word of God;
Have persecuted those who peaceably fear the Lord,
Have exiled them, deprived them of life
And property, made Widows and Orphans:
"Oh, revenge!" cries all that innocent blood.    Gen 4:10, 2
Esd 15:10

*[A letter from Maeyken de Corte]*

[2 Th 3:1] My dear Sister, pray for us, that the Word of the Lord may have free course and be fruitful, as we wait for him in complete equanimity and blissful contentment. [Rev 22:12] As he comes he will come and bring his reward with him; [1 Th 5:24] faithful is he, and he who has promised it will surely do it. For it is surely as I am saying: [Job 7:1] our life on earth is a constant battle.

You should know that I am in reasonable spirits, and my body is reasonably well, let the Lord be praised. [1 Cor 4:13] To be sure, here we are considered a curse to this world, [2 Cor 5:2] and always long passionately to be home, though we long for a home not constructed by human hands but for Heaven itself. [2 Pet 3:13] For we look for a new Heaven and a new Earth according to his promise, in which righteousness does dwell. How we will need to be suitable with a God-fearing being! I find I am often downcast, I also find so many shortcomings in myself, and so much that must yet die; I must give it all over to the Lord with a humble heart and a trembling, downcast spirit, and beseech him for mercy rather than justice. [1 Cor 1:27, Phil 2:12] I notice that the less I make of myself, the more our mighty God works in me and the more he pours his mercy over me: then I weep most bitterly and, falling on my knees, thank my God and say: "Oh my Lord and God, how much I am Adam's child! Yet you nevertheless remember him! You have given him glory above all your works! How is it that you visit us so abundantly, and so

en soo mildelijk uw schatten opent, en in ons laet ingaen en schijnen de schoone morgensterre in onse herten, [2.Pet.1.19., 2.Cor.4.6. ] ende hebt ons getrocken uyt dese donkere nacht, tot dat onvergankelijke licht, wat sullen wy hem wederom geven mijn lieve Suster, [Psal.51. 19.] dan een rouwig en verslagen herte en gebroken geest, met liefde en groote dankbaerheyd, daer rust den Geest des Heeren seyt David, laet ons malkanderen hertelijk lief hebben, [1.Joh. 4.8.] want God is de liefde, en malkanderen altijd vermanen, [Matt.24.12.] op dat wy niet verkouden, door 't bedrog der sonden, op dat God in ons geeert mag worden, [Hebr.3.13., 1.Thess.3.2] en dat wy verlost mogen worden van de hooveerdigheyd, en arge quade menschen, want het geloove is niet een yegelijks ding, [1.Cor.10.13.] de Heere is getrouw, dewelken ons sal sterken en bewaren.

Weet dat mijn Susters hier geweest hebben, en begeert een troostelijk woord van my te hebben, ende de Heere heeft noch de victorie behouden, ik weet niet wat van my is, ik heb'er geen trek toe, [Luc.14.26] al of sy my niet en bestonden, en ik kander my niet in verblijden, al is't dat ik se sie, en my dunkt dat se van my vervaert zijn: Sy maekten my soo vele kruycen, en hadden Balten een klooster-broeder hier gesonden te examineeren, en wilden hem wel drie kappen geven kost hy my bekeeren, hy quam aen met schoone woorden: maer ik wilde niet spreeken, en was toen sieck. Toen seyden mijn Susteren: Waerom spreekt gy niet? Toen seyde ik: Het lust my nu niet wel, wy hebben soo dikwils met hem gesprooken, hy weet onse mening wel.

Toen wierd Balten gram, en ging seer over my klagen, dat ik met kracht de Schrifture wederstaen hadde, en dat ik t'onrecht op de saligheyd stond, en dat ik geen hope hadde. Toen weenden sy seer, maer 't en ging my niet in, waer hy sweeg of sprak, hy dede al het volk uyt de kamer gaen, en liet mijn beyde mijn Susters, en hy en ik, en badt my seer, seggende: Mijn lieve Maeyken hebt medelijden met u arme ziele. Toen sprak ik kloekmoediglijk, so verhope ik ook te doen, en segt (seyden sy) dat het u leet is, en gy gedoolt hebt, het is genoeg, gy behoeft niet meer te seggen, men sal u terstond een cedulle maken na mijn hand, en ik sal se selve tekenen, en beyde de Schoonbroeders, het sal verborgen blijven, en men sal u al doen dat mogelijk is, laet dit geschieden mijn lieve Suster. Toen wierd ik beroert in mijn geest, en sprak: Gy meugt uw hooft wel rusten, gy doet al verloren moeyte, ik

generously open your treasures, allowing us to enter in? [2 Pet 1:19, 2 Cor 4:6] You cause the beautiful daystar to arise in our hearts, pulling us out of this dark night to that eternal light!" What can we give him in return, dear Sister, [Ps 51:17] other than a contrite and downcast heart and a broken spirit, with love and great thankfulness? "There the Spirit of the Lord does rest," says David. Let us love one another ardently, [1 Jn 4:8] for God is love, and admonish one another continually so that we do not grow cold [Mt 24:12] through the deceitfulness of sin. [Heb. 3:13] We do this so that God may be honored through us, and that we may be saved from pride and from iniquitous and evil people. For faith is not for everyone; the Lord is faithful, he will strengthen and preserve us. [2 Th 3:2, 1 Cor 10:13]

You should know that my Sisters were here, seeking a comforting word from me; in this the Lord did carry the victory. I don't know who is mine anymore, I have no need for them, [Lk 14:26] it's as though they no longer exist for me; I cannot be happy even though I see them, and I think they are frightened by me. They made so many signs of the cross over me, and had sent Balten, a monk, here to examine me; they would have given him at least three hoods if he were able to convert me! He came at me with beautiful words but I refused to talk, and then I became ill. Then my Sisters said: "Why don't you say anything?" I answered: "I don't feel like it right now, we have talked with him so often, he knows very well what we believe."

At that Balten flew into a rage and complained bitterly about me, how I had forcefully resisted the Scriptures, that I wrongly insisted on my salvation, and that I had no hope. They wept bitterly, but it did not touch me, regardless of whether he kept silent or spoke. He asked everyone to leave the room except for both my Sisters as well as he and I, and he beseeched me urgently, saying: "My dear Maeyken, have pity on your poor soul!" Then I answered stoutly: "That is exactly what I hope to do!" They said: "Just say that you are sorry, and that you have erred, that is enough, you don't have to say more; they will immediately make you a certificate on my authority, and I will personally sign it, and so will both your brothers-in-law. It will remain a secret, and everything possible will be done on your behalf. Let this happen, my dear sister!" Then I in my spirit became highly distressed and I said: "You might as well rest your mind, your efforts

ben van die mening niet, dat ik seggen sal dat het my leet soude sijn, het is my soo leet, had ik 't niet gedaen ik soude het noch doen, dat ik in mijnen sin hebbe, ik begeer daer in te blijven, [Phil.4.13.] met Gods hulpe, [Luc.14.26.] noch om bidden, noch om pijnen, [Rom.8.38.] noch om dood, noch om leven, 't en sal anders met my niet zijn, en ik begeere daer in te sterven. Aldus quelt my niet.

Ik wilde wel mocht het my gebeuren, dat ik Lauwerens Huysmaker spreeken mocht, en al u-lieden aensichten sien, maer ik moet lijdsaem wesen. [Luc.21.17., Act.20.21., Rom.16.] Blijft den Heere bevolen, en 't woord sijner genaden, groet my Andries, groet my Mattheus: Ik groete u beyden, groet my Lauwerens, groet my Hans, groet my Adriaen seer, en Lauwerens huysvrouw, en Lauwerens de Pesemakers Wijf, en Hanskens Wijf.

are all in vain. I do not believe that I will ever say that I should feel sorry, that I am sorry. If I hadn't done it yet I would do it now, that which I have resolved to do; I desire to remain steadfast in it, with the help of God. Neither prayer, nor torture, nor death, nor life [Phil 4:13, Lk 14:26, Rom 8:38] will make me think differently, and I wish to die in this belief. So don't torment me anymore."[5]

What I would like, if it were possible, would be to speak to Lauwerens Huysmaker, and to see all of your faces, but I must be patient. [Lk 21:17 (?), Acts 20:21 (?), Rom. 16] I once again commend you to the Lord, and to the message of his mercy. Greet Andries for me, greet Matthew for me, I greet you both; greet Lauwerens for me, greet Hans for me, greet Adriaen especially, and the wife of Lauwerens, and the wife of Lauwerens the Cord-maker, and the wife of Hansken.

[5] According to the punctuation of the Netherlandic text, this sentence and the following are one, which is problematic: does Maeyken say to the addressee of the letter: "Don't torment me", or to Balten that she would like to see Lauwerens Huysmaker and other fellow believers? It makes more sense to consider the Netherlandic punctuation in error, and to separate the phrases as we have done in the translation.

# MARTHA BAERTS

*Aen mijn Suster Betken. Een schoen Geestelick Liedeken, ghemaeckt door die selve Vrouwe Soetken vanden Houten Haer Maecht Martha.*

Op die Wijse: wel hem de Godes vrede staet.

Melody: Souterliedeken 99

1.     O Godt ghy zijt mijn Hulper fijn
        Verlost my van de eewige pijn
        O Heere wilt my bewaeren,
        Voor den Draec met zijn scharen.

2.     O Godt ghy zijt mijn toeverlaet
        Daer alle mijnen sin op staet,
        O Heere wilt my behouwen,
        Op u staet mijn betrouwen.

# MARTHA BAERTS
(beheaded November 20, 1560, in Ghent)

*To my Sister Betken.*[1] *A lovely Spiritual Song, made by the Maid Martha of this same Lady Soetken van den Houte*

To the Tune: "Blest he, who has the peace of God"

1    O God, thou art my Helper good,
Preserve me from eternal pain;
O Lord, I pray thee to protect me
From the Dragon and his hosts!

2    O God, thou art my refuge,
My heart is fixed on thee;
O Lord, I pray thee, keep me safe,
I put my trust in thee.

---

[1] "To my Sister Betken" is on the bottom of the previous page, after the end of Soetken's many adieus. While it most logically belongs with Martha's song, it is curious that it was not placed at the beginning of the next page with the title there; there would have been enough room in the pamphlet, for the last stanza of Martha's song stands alone on the last page.

3   Mijn verlosser is Godt alleyn,
    Maeckt my van alle sonden reyn,
    Ende wiltse doch my vergeven,
    Opdat ick mach eewich leven.

4   Het vleisch doet mi so groet gequel
    Twederstaet wat die Heere wil,
    O Heere wilt mijns ghedencken,
    Mijn lichaem wil ick u schenken.

5   Mijn Sonden syn sonder getal,
    O Heere wiltse my vergheven al,
    Wilt mijn ellende aenschouwen,
    Ende met uwen Geest bedouwen.

6   Die verleyders quellen my so seer
    Om my te trecken van Godes leer
    Die en wil ick niet ghelooven,
    Want sy soecken my te verdooven.

7   Mijn Vrienden doen my ooc vermaen
    Dat ick soude mijn Geloof afgaen,
    O neen dat wil ick behouwen,
    Totter doot al sonder flouwen.

8   Doe seyden sy al metter spoet,
    Daeromme sult ghy inder hellen gloet
    Dat eewige Vyer beerven,
    Het Rijcke Godts sult ghy derven.

9   Doe seyde ic haer met koelen moe,
    Dit Oordel hoort den Heere toe,
    Hoe derft ghy dat uut spreken,
    Het quaet sal hy wel wreecken.

10  Doe seyden sy du snoode Beest,
    In Oudenaerde is noyt geweest,
    Gheene so quaet bevonden
    Van sulcken boosen gronden.

3   My saviour, he is God alone,
    From all my sins does wash me clean,
    I pray thee, do forgive them me,
    So I may live eternally.

4   My flesh torments me greatly,
    Opposes the Lord's good will.
    O Lord, wilt thou remember me,
    My body will I give to thee.

5   Without number are my Sins,
    O Lord, wilt thou forgive them all,
    Wilt thou observe my misery,
    And with thy Spirit them bedew.

6   The tempters torment me so much
    To separate me from God's creed;
    But yet, believe them I will not,
    For to ruin me they seek.

7   My Friends, too, do admonish me,
    That my faith I should renounce;
    Oh no! to that I will hold fast,
    Up until death - I will not flag!

8   Next they said, with sharp impatience:
    "For that you will in hell's hot glow,
    Earn that everlasting Fire,
    And God's Kingdom you'll forgo!"

9   I answered them, in spirit calm:
    "Such Judgement is the Lord's alone.
    How dare you utter loud such thoughts?
    Most surely evil he'll avenge!"

10  Then they replied: "You lowly Beast!
    In Oudenaard' there's never been
    Anyone so wicked found
    With such an evil core!"

11   Al versmaet my de werelt quaet,
     Die Heere is mijn toeverlaet,
     Ick hoope hy sal my stercken,
     Ende crachtich met my wercken.

12   Och Broeders ende Susters fyn
     Laet ons altijt gedachtich syn,
     Den Heere der Heerscharen,
     Hy sal ons altijt bewaren.

13   Ick bidde al die hooren dit Liedt
     En wilt u doch verschricken niet
     Het cruyce te aenveerden,
     Godt kan ons helpen volherden.

14   Die dit Liedeken heeft gemaeckt
     By die Blindeleiders is sy geraect
     Sy en brochtense niet gevanghen
     Maer quam van haer selfs gegangen.

     FINIS.

11   And should the evil world despise me,
     The Lord, he will my refuge be.
     I trust that he will strengthen me
     And work in me so powerfully.

12   Oh Brethren, Sisters, good and fine,
     Let us always mindful be
     Of the Lord of Hosts,
     He will always keep us.

13   I pray all those who hear this Song,
     Pray, do not be frightened off
     From taking on the cross:
     God can help us to endure.

14   The one who this Song did write,
     Arrived at those Leaders Blind;
     Not as a captive was she brought,
     But of her own free will she came.

## SOETKEN van den HOUTE

*En Testament, gemaeckt by Soetken van den Houte, het welcke sy binnen Gendt in Vlaenderen metten Doodt bevesticht heeft, Anno. M.D. ende LX den xxvij. Novenbris, Ende haeren kinderen David, Betken ende Tanneken tot een Memorie ende voor het alder beste Goet heeft naghelaten, Als een jegelick Leesen mach.*

Och mijn lieve kinderkens dit hebbe ic geschreven met tranen, u lieden vermanende uut liefden, met een vierich herte, voor u biddende, oft mogelic waer, dat ghy van dit geval bevonden mocht worden, want als uwen vader my ontnomen was, so en hebbe ic my selven niet ghespaert, dach noch nacht, om u lieden op te brengen, ende mijn Gebet ende sorge was altijt om uwer salicheydt, ende noch binnen bande zijnde, heeft dat altijt mijn meeste sorge gheweest, om dat ic u na mijn voorsicticheit niet beter beschicken konste, want als my gheseydt was, dat ghy na Oudenarden ende van daer na Brugge gheleydt waert, dat viel my so swaer, dat ick gheen meerder droeffenisse ghehadt en hebbe, Maer als ick dachte, dat mijn sorghe oft beschicken niet helpen en mocht, ende datmen scheyden moet, van alle datmen lief heeft in dese wereldt om Christus wille, soe hebbe ic dat al inden wille des HEEREN ghestelt hoopende noch altijt ende biddende, dat hy u lieden bewaren wil in zijnder bermherticheydt, ghelijck hy Joseph, Moysen, ende Daniel bewaerde, onder die Godtloose Minschen, ende het sal u alsoo gheluckende, ist dat ghy u beneerstiget te schicken na die waerheydt, soo sal die Enghel des Heeren met u zijn [Tobi.6., Dani.13.], ghelijck hy was met Tobias, hem leydende, tot dat hy hem brochte in zijns Vaders huys, daer hy hem verblijde met zijnen Vader ende vrienden, Godt danckende van zijnder grooter goetheydt.[...]

David mijn lieve Kindt, ick wil u hier mede den HEERE bevelen, ghy zijt die Outste, leert wysheyt, op dat ghy u Susterkens goet Exempel gheeft, ende wacht u van quaede Geselschap, ende van achter straten te spellen met de quade knechten, maer leert seer leesen ende schryven, op dat ghy verstandich wordt, ende hebt

# SOETKEN van den HOUTE
## (beheaded November 20, 1560 in Ghent)

*A Testament made by Soetken van den Houte, which she confirmed with her death in Ghent in Flanders, in the year 1560, the 27<sup>th</sup> of November,*[1] *and left as a memorial for her children David, Betken, and Tanneken, as well as for the greater Good, as anyone can read* (excerpts)*:*

[...] Oh, my dear little children! I wrote this in tears, admonishing you out of love, with a passionate heart praying for you that it might be possible that you experience this blessed state as well. For when your father was taken from me, I did not spare myself, neither day nor night, to raise you; and my prayer and care was always for your salvation. And even now, while imprisoned, it was always my greatest worry that despite my vigilance I could not arrange things better for you: for when they told me that you had been taken to Oudenaarde and from there to Bruges, that was so hard for me that I have not had greater sorrow. But when I remembered that my worry or arrangements would not help, and that for Christ's sake it is necessary to part from all that one loves in this world, so I put this whole matter into the will of the LORD. All the while I hope and pray that he will keep you all in his mercy, just as he kept Joseph, Moses, and Daniel while they were among Godless People. And you will similarly succeed, if indeed you apply yourselves to being faithful to the Truth. Then the Angel of the Lord will be with you [Tob 6, Dan 3], as he was with Tobias, leading him until he brought him into his Father's house, where he rejoiced with his Father and friends, thanking God for his great goodness [...]

David, my dear Child, with this I want to commend you to the LORD. You are the Eldest: acquire wisdom so that you may set your little Sisters a good example; guard yourself against bad Companions, and against playing with bad fellows in back alleys. Rather, learn to read and write well, so that you may become wise. Love

---

[1] The pamphlet gives the date of November 27, which is wrong, as other records show that Soetken and two other women (including Martha Baerts) were beheaded on November 20 (for a precise account of their imprisonment and execution, see Gregory, "Soetken").

malcanderen lief, sonder twist oft ghekijff, maer zijt vriendelick die een den anderen, den wysten sal den slechsten verdraeghen, ende vermanen met vriendelicheydt, den stercken sal metten krancken medelyden hebben, ende helpen hem al dat hy kan uut liefden, den rijcken sal den armen bystandt doen, uut Broederlicke Liefde, die Jonckste sal den Oudtsten gehoorsaem zijn in het ghoede, [...]

Voort mijn lieve Kint Betken, ende Tanneken, mijn lieve schaepkens, ick vermane u lieden in al dit selve, als dat ghy ghehoorsaem wilt zijn den Gheboden des Heeren [Deu.6., Psal.19., 119.], ende voort u Oomken ende Moeyken ghehoorsaem zijt, ende voort u Ouders, ende alle die u totter duecht onderwijsen, dies Broot dat ghy eet, moet ghy onderdanich zijn, in al dat teghen God niet en is, ende zijt neerstich u selven altijt vermanende om u werck te doen, soo salmen u lief hebben, waer dat ghy woonen, ende zijt niet kijfachtich, noch clapachtich noch lichtveerdich, noch stoudt, noch stuer van spreecken, maer vriendelick, eerlijck ende stille, ghelijck die jonghe Dochteren toe behoort, bidt den HEEre om wijsheyt, u sal gegheven woorden, leert seer leesen ende schrijven, neempt u ghenoechte daer in, soo sult ghy wijss worden, neemt u genoechte ende bekummeringhe met Psalmen, Loffsanghen, ende Gheestelijcke Liedekens [Psal.6., Collo.3.], staet nae die eenige vruecht, leert den Heere behaghen van uwer Jonckheydt aen, alsoo die Heylighe Vrouwen ende Dochters ghedaen hebben. Gelyck Judith. Ende Hester was een Dochter die Godt vreesde, vercierde met ootmoedicheydt, Gracelick, Eeerlick Vriendelick ende Vernedert van herten, ende daerom heeft sy den Coeninck Achasverus behaecht, booven alle andere Dochteren, Maer in haeren Staet en was sy niet hooveerdich, al wast dat sy met Coninclicke Cleederen blinckte, soo heeft sy haer vernedert, met vasten ende bidden, tot den HEEre voor haer Broeders dat sy mochten verlosset worden, uut haerder Vyanden handen, haer selven niet hooger achtende, dan eene vanden minsten van haren Broederen. [...]

Min lieve Kinderkens, dit laet ick u tot een ghedachtenisse oft Testament, ist dat ghyt ter winninge legt, ghy sulter meerder Schat mede vergaderen, dan oft ick u veel Rijcdommen achter gelaten hadde, dat verganckelick is, Want men can het Goedt van der werlt verliesen door Brant, Oorloge, oft mal Fortuyn. daeromme en is hy niet

one another without fighting or quarreling, rather be kind to one another. Let the wisest tolerate the most foolish and admonish with gentleness; the strong shall have compassion for the weak and in love help him all that he can; the rich shall assist the poor in Brotherly Love, the Youngest shall obey the Eldest in what is good. [...]

Further, my dear Child Betken, and Tanneken: my dear little sheep, I admonish you both in the same things, that you may obey the Commandments of the Lord [Dt 6, Ps 19, 119]. Further, I admonish you to obey your Uncle and Auntie, and also your Elders and all those who instruct you in virtue. Whoever gives you your Bread you must obey in all that is not against God; be industrious, always admonishing yourselves to do your work, for then you will be loved wherever you may live. And do not be quarrelsome, nor gossipy, nor flighty, nor naughty, nor impolite in your talk, but be friendly, honest and calm, as suits young Daughters. Pray to the LORD for wisdom, it will be given you; learn to read and write well, and if you take pleasure in that, then you will become wise. Take your pleasure and your leisure from Psalms, Hymns of Praise, and Spiritual Songs, [Ps 66 (?)[2]]. Pursue that one and only joy, [Col 3] learn to please the Lord from your Youth, as did the Holy Women and Daughters, like Judith. And Esther was a Daughter who feared the Lord, adorned with humility, Graceful, Honest, Kind, and Lowly of heart; that is why she pleased King Ahasuerus more than all other Daughters. But despite her State she was not proud; even though she stood out in her Royal Robes she humbled herself through fasting and praying to the LORD on behalf of her Brethren, that they might be saved from the hands of their Enemies, not considering herself better than one of the least of these her Brethren. [...]

My dear little Children, I leave you this as a remembrance or Testament; if you invest it advantageously, you will gain greater Treasure with it than if I had left you great Riches that are mortal. For one can lose the Goods of this world through Fire, War, or bad Fortune; therefore he

---

[2] The reference to Ps 6 in the original is clearly not correct; Ps 66 does begin with the well known injunction to "make a joyful noise" to God. "Psalms, hymns, and spiritual song" is a quote from Eph 5:19.

wijss, de zijn herte stel op yet dat verganckelick is, want wy niet een ure tijdts versekerheydt en hebben, wy moetent alle achterlaten, daerom en zijt niet droeve, all ist dat het selve, dat wy hadden verstroyt, oft verlooren is, als Paulus seyt: wy moeten allemans Roof zijn, daerom moet ghy noch den Heere dancken, dat hi ons gelaeten heeft, tot dat ick u dus verre opgebracht hebbe, ende ist dat ghy in alder Gherechticheyt wandelen soo sal u die Heere genoch verleenen neempt een exempel aen Tobias. [Psa.36.] ende David die seyt: Dat die gherechtighe gheen ghebreck hebben en sal, noch zijn Saedt omme broot gaen.[...]

Hiermede wil ick u lieden Adieu seggen Adieu mijn lieve kinderkens ende Adieu mijn lieve Vrienden altesamen.[...]

Hiermede seg ick Adieu, mijn lieve kint Betken, Adieu mijn lieve kinderkens David ende Tanneken, Adieu mijn lieve Broeders ende Susters alle tesamen, Vrienden overalle.

Noch segghen wy eens Adieu, groet my Oomken ende Moyken seere, mit eenen kus des vredes uut mynen Naeme. Geschreven by my Soetken van den Houte, u Moeder in banden. geschreven mit haesten (al bevende van coude) uut liefden van u lieder allen Amen.

is not wise who sets his heart on anything that is mortal. For we are not assured about even one hour, we have to leave all behind. Therefore do not be sorrowful, even if those things that we had are dispersed or lost; as Paul says: "We must all be everyone's Prey." Therefore you should still thank the Lord that he has left us until I could raise you thus far. And if you walk in the ways of all Righteousness, the Lord will grant you sufficiency; take Tobias as an example, as well as David who said: "The righteous will not suffer lack, nor his Offspring beg for bread [Ps 37:25]." [...]

With this I want to bid you all Adieu; Adieu, my dear little children, and Adieu my dear friends, all of you.

[*Another letter follows, with this closing:*] With this I say Adieu, my dear child Betken; Adieu, my dear children David and Tanneken; Adieu my dear Brothers and Sisters all, Friends everywhere.

Yet once more we say Adieu; greet Uncle and Auntie heartily for me with a kiss of peace in my name. Written by me, Soetken van den Houte, your imprisoned mother, in haste (and shivering with cold), in love to all of you. Amen.

# MAYKEN BOOSERS

*Noch eenen Brief aan haer Ouders.*

Uut dat binnenste mijnder herten groete ick u, mijn beminde vader ende mijn seer gelievede moeder, met alle de gene die binnen uwen huyse zijn, u sal believen te weten, dat ick gesont ende onverandert van gemoede ben, de Heere sy eewich gheloeft, alsoo verhoepe ick door Godts goetheyt, dattet met u oock staet. Voort so dancke ick u hertelijc van uwe vriendelijcke groetenisse, aen my gheschreven, waer van ick my seer verblijt hebbe, hoorende u ghemoet ende goede gonste, ende om der ghedachtenisse, soo wil ic u wat van mijn gevanckenisse schrijven.

Ten eersten, heeft my die Commissarius ghevraecht, hoe out dat ick was doen ick ghedoopt worde. Ick seyde: Ontrent 23. oft 24. Jaer. Sy vraechden, waerom ick dat hadde laten doen. Ick seyde: [Mar.16. b.15.] Om dat het God bevolen hadde. Sy vraechden, oft ick niet en wiste dat ick te voren al gedoopt was. Ick seyde: Ick en weet daer niet af, oock en heeft God sulcks niet bevolen. Sy vraechden, oft ick gheen Peters noch Meters gehadt en hadde. Ick sprac: Het mach wel zijn, sy mogen gestorven zijn. Doen seyden sy, men soude my Geleerden senden. Ic seyde: Ghy behoort wijs ghenoech te zijn, om tegen my te spreken, maer sy wouden Geleerder senden. Daer na hebben sy den Prochepape vande vrouwen Kercke gesonden, die quam aen ende seyde, waerom ick so langhe in zijn Kercke niet gheweest en hadde, ende dat hy gheen kennisse van my ghehadt en hadde. Ick seyde, dat ick my stillekens in huys gehouden hadde. Sy vraechden, waer mijn Kercke

# MAYKEN BOOSERS
(burned September 18, 1564, in Doornik)

*In addition, a letter to her Parents:*[1]

From the depths of my heart do I greet you, my cherished father and my dearly beloved mother, and all those who are within your house. You will be pleased to hear that I am healthy and constant in spirit, the Lord be eternally praised - and I hope through God's goodness that the same is true for you. Further, I thank you heartily for your friendly greetings written to me, which brought me great joy, hearing how you were and of your good affections. In as a token of remembrance I want to write you something of my imprisonment.

First, the Commissar asked me how old I was when I was baptized. I said: "About 23 or 24." They asked why I had had that done. I said, [Mk 16:16] because God had commanded it. They asked whether I didn't know that I had been baptized already. I said: "I don't know anything about that, and besides, God did not command that." They asked whether I had neither godfather nor godmother. I said: "It could be, maybe they've died." Then they said that they would send some Learned men to me. I said: "You ought to be wise enough to speak with me"; but they insisted on sending someone more Learned. Then they sent the Parish Priest of the Church of Our Lady; he arrived and asked why I had not been in his Church for such a long time, and said that he had no knowledge of me. I replied that I had been keeping myself quietly at home. They asked where my Church

---

[1] *Het Offer* begins with Mayken's brief confession (not included here), in which she tells also of her shame at being undressed by her torturers, and how she undresses herself; in one letter to "the Brethren" (also not included) Mayken reports of moving her inquisitors to tears, a detail included in the song (stanza 14). Excerpts from the letters have been chosen to reveal Mayken's warm love and concern for her family as well as her steadfast and clearly articulated faith; compared to some of the others, Mayken describes her experiences briefly and almost dispassionately, with relatively little directly reported dialogue, indicating that she was indeed "whiling away her time," as she says, before she would die for her faith as she longed to do. There is a minor discrepancy in the report of her date of death: according to *Het Offer* it was September 18, while a letter from Mayken's grandson, Jan de Booser, talks of September 10 (Cramer, *Het Offer*, 411).

was. Ic seyde: Sy was haer onbekent, want waert dat ghyse wistet, ghy en soutse niet langer met vreden laten. Wy hadden tsamen veel woorden vanden Doop. Ic seyde, [Mat.28.c.19.] dat Christus zijn Apostolen uutgesonden hadde in alle de werelt, ende leeren eerst alle volcken onderhouden, al dat hy haer bevolen hadde, ende haer doopen inden naem des Vaders, des Soons des heyligen Geests. [Mar.16.b.15.] Geen kinderen en connen leeren, maer wie gelooft ende ghedoopt wort, sal salich wesen. Doen seyden sy, [1.Cor.16.] dat de Apostolen heele Huysghesinnen hadden gedoopt. Ick seyde: Ja, dan hebben sy haer verblijt datse in God gheloovich waren geworden, dat en conden de kinderen niet doen, God heeft de kinderen tot hem gheroepen, ende heeft geseyt, [Math.19.d.] dat alsodanigen dat Hemelrijck toebehoort, maer hy en bevalse niet om te doopen. Daer quamen sy voort met Adams sonde, hoe dat sy daer in gheboren waren. Ick seyde, dat Christus daer voor ghestorven waer. Ick vraechde haerlieden, oft sy de sonde met den Doop wouden afdoen, [Luce.9.e., Rom.6.a.4.] want de jonghe kinderen doch gheen sonde en hebben, daerom en connen sy de sonden niet sterven, ende verrijsen door dat Doopsel in een nieu leven. Doen seyden de Heeren: U seggen is: Wie ghelooft ende gedoopt wordt, sal salich wesen, ist niet? Ick seyde: Jae.

Doen vraechden sy, oft Christus niet van Maria vleesch en ware. Ick seyde, dat hem Maria vanden heylighen Gheest ontfanghen hadde, ghelijck de Engel tot haer sprack: De heylige Gheest sal van boven in u comen, ende de cracht des Alderhoochsten sal u omschijnen, daeromme dat Heylighe dat van u gheboren sal worden, sal Godts Sone ghenaemt worden. Sy seyden noch eens, oft hy van haer gheen vleesch aengenomen en hadde, nadenmael hy van boven niet ghebrocht en hadde. Ick seyde, dat ick Joannis getuychenisse wel geloofde, daer hy seyt: [Joan.1.a.13.] Dat woort is vleesch geworden ende heeft onder ons gewoont. Sy vraechden oft ick niet en geloofde, dat hy Marien Sone na den vleesche is, ende Gods Sone na den Geest. Ick seyde, dat hy Gods eyghen geboren ende eenige geboren Sone is, die van [Heb.7.a.4.] begin der dagen, sonder eynde des levens is, ende nu ten laetsten, so is hy door des heylighen Geests cracht van Maria geboren, [Luce.1.c.32.] Daerom en is hy niet vander aerden, aertsch gelijck Adam, ende en sal ooc niet tot Aerde keeren, want hy is de Heere vanden Hemel, ende hadde hi nu vleesch van onsen vleesche, so moeste hy ooc de verganckelijcheyt sien, want God sprack: [Gen.3.d.20.] Ghy zijt Aerde ende sult weder tot aerde keeren, dan dat en was niet alleen van Adam, maer alle die van hem af quamen.

was. I said that it would be unknown to them, "for if you knew where it was, you wouldn't leave it in peace any longer." We exchanged many words about Baptism. I said [Mt 28:19] that Christ had sent his Apostles out into all the world, to first teach all nations to observe all that he had commanded them, and then to baptize them in the name of the Father, the Son, and the Holy Ghost. [Mk 16:16] No children can receive such knowledge, but whoever believes and is baptized shall be saved. Then they said [1 Cor 1:16] that the Apostles had baptized entire Households. I said: "Yes, then they were gladdened that they had come to believe in God, but children were not able to do that. God called the little children to him and said [Mt 19:14] that to such belongs the Kingdom of Heaven, but he did not command that they be baptized." Then they brought up Adam's sin, how children were born into sin. I said that Christ had died for that. I asked them whether they would remove sin through baptism, for, after all, little children have no sin [Lk 9:48 (?)] and therefore they cannot die to sin and rise through Baptism into new life [Rom 6:4]. Then the Magistrates said: "Don't you say: 'whoever believes and is baptized shall be saved'?" I said: "Yes."

Next they asked whether Christ was born of the flesh of Mary. I said that Mary had conceived him through the Holy Ghost, as the angel spoke to her: "The Holy Ghost shall come from on high upon you, and the power of the Most High shall shine about you, so that the Holy One who shall be born from you shall be called the Son of God." They asked again whether he had not taken on mortal flesh from her, considering he had not brought it from on high. I said that I believed completely the testimony of John, where he says: [Jn 1:14] "The word has become flesh and dwelt among us." They asked whether I didn't believe that he was Mary's Son according to the flesh, and God's Son according to the Spirit. I answered that he was God's own and only born Son, who is from the [Heb 7:3] beginning of time and without end of life, and, as last point, so he was born of Mary through the power of the Holy Ghost [Lk 1:31]. Hence he is not of this earth, mortal like Adam, and will also not return to Earth, for he is the Lord of heaven. And if he did indeed have flesh according to our flesh, he would also have to see death, for God spoke: [Gen 3:19] "Dust you are and to dust you shall return," and that was not only for Adam but all his descendants.

Doen vraechden sy my, oft ick niet en geloofde, dat int Sacrament Christus vleesch ende bloet ware. Ic seyde: [Mar.16.c.16., Act.7.g.56.] Neen, hy is opgeclommen, ende sit ter rechterhant Godts zijns Vaders. Doen vraechden sy, oft ic niet en wilde gelooven, dat alle de Heyligen inden Hemel zijn. Ic seyde: Dat ick niet gelesen en hebbe, en can ic niet verantwoorden, mer aldus vele heb ic gelesen: [Sap.5.a.1.] De gerechtige sielen zijn inde handen Gods, [Apo.21.a.4] ende de pijne des doots en salse niet aenroeren. Daer en seydense doen niet veel op, Mer sy vraechden, wat ic hielde van Maria. Ic seyde, dat[Luce.1.b.24.] sy een suyver ende een heylich vat was, ende gebenedijt boven alle vrouwen want sy was weerdich den Soone Gods te ontfangen ende baren. Sy vraechden, oft ic niet en bekende, datter een Vagevyer is. Ic seyde: Van twee wegen vinde ick geschreven, [Mat.7.b.14.] de eene seer breet totter verdoemenisse, dander seer smal tot het eewige leven leydende. Noch vraechden sy, wat ic vanden Paus hielt. Ic sprac: Den Paus en kenne ic niet, maer isset zijn leeringe diemen hier hout, so houde ic hem zijnder leeringe gelijck. Daer hebben veel meer woorden gheweest, maer dese schrijve ick uut tijtcortinghe. Vaert alle wel.

*Een Testament aen haer kinderen.*

Een hertelijcke ende gonstige groete sy aen u lieden geschreven, mijn beminde kinderen, u moeder die nu om de rechte waerheyt in banden is, wilt doch hooren, want het heeft God also behaecht, [2.Tim.3.b.12.] dat alle die godsalich willen leven moeten vervolginge lijden, Dus ben ic wel te vreden ende getroost, [Mat.10.c.25.] dat de knecht zijnen Heere na volcht, [Luc.11.a.2.] zijnen gebenedijden wille moet met my geschieden, haddet hem belieft, hy soude dese banden wel belet hebben. Mijn lieve kinderen, het heeft vanden beginne also geweest, dat de gerechtige lijden moesten, [Gene.4.b.9., Luc.23.c.20.] ende de ongerechtige altijt de overhant, maer haren dach sal haest comen, [Apo.6.c.16.] datse beclaghen sullen, ende van ellende roepen: Bergen valt op ons, ende Huevelen bedeckt ons voor het aensicht des Heeren. [...]

Ic bidde u mijn lieve kinderen, weest doch vreetsaem onder malcanderen, dat is een vruecht des Geests, helpt malcanderen gewillich sonder eenich tegenspreken, ende weest altijt den armen gedachtich, [Heb.13.c.10.] geeft willich van allen dat ghi hebt maect u vrienden vanden ongerechtigen Mammon, bemint dat eewich

Then they asked me whether I didn't believe that Christ's flesh and blood were present in the Sacraments. I said: [Mk 16:19, Acts 7:56] "No, he has ascended into heaven, and sits at the right hand of God his Father." Then they asked me if I wouldn't believe that all of the Saints are in Heaven. I replied I couldn't give an account of that which I hadn't read anywhere, but that I had read this: [Wis 3:1, Rev 21:4] "The souls of the righteous are in the hands of God, and the torment of death shall not touch them." They didn't say a lot to that, but they asked what I believed about Mary. I answered that [Lk 1:42] she was a pure and holy vessel, blessed above all women, for she was worthy to conceive and bear the Son of God. They asked whether I didn't confess that there was a Purgatory. I said: "I find written of two roads, [Mt 7:14] the one very broad, leading to damnation, the other very narrow, leading to eternal life." Finally they asked what I believed about the Pope. I said: "I do not know the Pope, but if the doctrine they hold to here is his, I hold him to be like his doctrine." A lot more words were used, but I write you these to while away the time. Farewell, all of you.

*A Testament to her children* (excerpts):

Let a heartfelt and affectionate greeting be written to you, my dear children, from your mother who is now imprisoned for the sake of upright truth; do heed me, for it has pleased God [2 Tim 3:12] that all those who would live a godly life must suffer persecution. And so I am very satisfied and comforted, [Mt 10:25] for the servant follows his Master; [Lk 11:2] his blessed will must be done with me: if it had pleased him, he would have hindered this imprisonment. My dear children, it has been so from the beginning that the just must suffer [Gen 4:9, Lk 23:20] and the unjust always have the upper hand; but their day will soon come [Rev 6:16] that they will weep, and call out in misery: "Mountains fall on us, and hills cover us from the face of the Lord!" [...]

I pray you, my dear children, live in harmony with one another, for that is a fruit of the Spirit; help one another willingly and without any objections. Always remember the poor, [Heb 13:16] give willingly of all that you have; do not become lovers of Mammon[2]; choose your friends

---

[2] The Dutch text is unclear: "maect u vrienden vanden ongerechtigen Mammon" would be most correctly translated as "become friends of the unrighteous Mammon." We have interpreted the text as missing the negative ("maect u *geen* vrienden vanden...") it has in some scriptural references to Mammon (e.g. 1 Tim 3:3).

is, ende niet dat tijtlijc is, [Collo.3.a.2.]soect dat Hemels, ende niet dat aertsch is, [1.Pe.1.d.24.] want alle vleesch is als gras, ende de heerlijcheyt des menschen als een bloeme des gras, dat heden staet ende morgen inden oven geworpen wort, de heerlijcheyt des menschen vergaet, maer twoort des Heeren blijft eewich, en bemint niet de werelt, noch de dingen die daer in zijn, [Joan.2.c.16.] te weten, den lust der oogen, den homoet des levens, twelc niet en is van God maer vander werelt, ende de werelt sal vergaen met al dat daer in is, mer die den wille des Vaders doet, [1.Cor.7.c.31.] die blijft inder eewicheyt.

Mijn kinderen, doet na des Heeren wille, ic u moeder, hope u den wech voor te gaen, merct waer in, ende hoe ic u voorgae, en wilt niet op des werelts eere sien, mer achtet eere te wesen om den naem ons Gods te lijden.[1.Pe.4.c.14., Phil.2.a.7.] Want hy die de alderopperste Coninc was, heeft hem niet geschaemt zijn heerlijcheyt te verlaten, ende is inder werelt gecomen, ende heeft den alder versmaetsten doot voor ons geleden, ende is sonder schult geslagen ende mismaect, dat daer niet geheels aen zijn gebenedijde lichaem was. So lief heeft hy ons gehadt, ende daer mede ons een exempel achtergelaten, op dat wy zijn voetstappen sullen na gaen. Hy is dat licht dat in de werelt gecomen is, op dat alle die hem navolghen, niet in duysternisse en souden wandelen, maer dat licht des levens hebben: De Heere beschicke, dat u dat selve licht ooc omschijne, ende ghy daer in wandelt. Amen

*Een Briefken vanden kinderen an haer moeder, bedankende haer onderwijs.*

Onse onderdanige, goetgonstige groete sy aen u geschreven lieve Moeder, wy gebieden ons onderdaenichlijck tuwaert, ende zijn u grootelick bedanckende van u goede onderwysinge, dat ghy ons gesonden hebt, ende wy hoopen ons daer nae te voegen ende te schicken, oock om vredelick met malcander tleven, achtervolgende u bevel, ende wy zyn dagelicx voor u biddende, dat Godt geve in u dat alderbeste dat u siele salich soude moegen zijn. Hier mede zijn wy u den Heere bevelende, de verleene u zijn eewige ruste, daer boven in zijn rycke, daer wy hopen by u te comen, God sy met u tot opten ander tijt.

from among those who do not serve Mammon; love what is eternal, and not what is mortal [Col 3:2]. Seek that which is Heavenly, and not that which is earthly, [1 Pet 1:24] for all flesh is as grass, and the splendor of man is as the flower of the grass, that today grows and tomorrow is cast into the oven: the splendor of man passes away, but the word of the Lord remains eternal. Do not love the world, or the things that are in it, [1 Jn 2:16] to wit the lust of the eye, the pride of life, which is not of God but of the world; the world shall pass away with all that is in it [1 Cor 7:31], but he who does the will of the Father shall live eternally.

My children, act according to the Lord's will. I, your mother, hope to travel this road before you: note in what way, and in what manner, I go before you, and do not attend to the honor of this world, but consider it an honor to suffer for the name of our God [1 Pe 4:14]. For he who was the most high King was not ashamed to leave his glory [Phil 2:7] and came into the world; he suffered the most shameful death for us, and without fault was beaten and mistreated, so that nothing remained whole in his blessed body. Thus dearly did he love us, and through this left us an example so that we might follow in his footsteps. He is the light that has come into the world, so that all who follow him should not walk in darkness but have the light of life. The Lord grant that that same light shine around about you, and that you walk in it. Amen.

*A Note from the children to their mother, thanking for her instruction:*[3]

Our obedient, sympathetic greetings be written to you, dear Mother; we commend ourselves obediently to you, and are greatly thankful to you for the good instruction which you sent us. We hope to abide by it and conform ourselves to it, also to live in harmony with one another, following your command. We pray for you daily, that God will give you the very best so that your soul might be saved. With this we commend you to the Lord, that he may grant you his eternal rest up above in his kingdom; we hope to come to you there. God be with you until another time.

[3] This note from the 1566 edition of *Het Offer*, left out in subsequent editions, is the only note we have by children to a parent, though we know that more were written. Its stylistic formality, even stiffness, seems typical for a child's way of writing letters, but their longing and affection does shine through. Cramer included the note in his edition of *Het Offer*, 626.

*Noch een Briefken van dese selve Moeder aen haer kinderen.*

Mijn kinderen, ic groet u seer hertelijc, ende sende u lieder geschriften wederom, op dat ghy u Belofte muecht quijten, die ghy my daer in gedaen hebt, ende weest doch altijt onderdanich, die u onderwijsen tot gerechticheyt, ende straffen in u overtredinghe. Vaert wel, ende hier mede op deser Werelt Adieu, mijn lieve kinderen, vreest Godt, schouwet alle quaet.

*Noch eenen Brief aen de Vrienden.*

Och mijn hertgrontlijcke, ende seer beminde B. ende S. inden Heere, ic groet u noch eens met des Heeren vrede, de selve by u te blijven tot inder eewicheyt, Amen.

Ick late u weten, hoe dat dese mijn vianden my noch altijt quellende blijven van het Doopsel, maer van de Menschwerdinghe Christi en seggense my niet, de Deecken verhaelde haer mijn gheloove, ende en vraechden my niet, dan oft ick oock gheloofde, dat Christus Davids Sone was. Ick seyde, [Mat.16.c.16.] dat hy de levendighe Gods Soone was. Och, och, sprack de Deecken. De Heeren vraechden: Stater niet geschreven uten Zade Davids na den vleesche [Act.13.c.23.]? De Deecken antwoorde haer, want daer en was gheen gehoor, hij hiet my dicmael liegen, om dat ic hem wederstont, dat hy my niet betogen en conde, dat de Apostolen kinderen gedoopt hadden. Sy overvielen my alle gelijc, ende spraken, datter niemant int Hemelrijc comen en mochte, ten waer dat hy geboren worde uut den water ende Geest. [Joann.3.a.6] Sy vraechden my metter haest, oft ic sulcx ooc niet en bekende. Ic seyde: De schrift en coemt den kinderen niet toe, maer den ouden, die daer ooren hebben om te hooren. Doen stonden sy op, ende seyden: Ghy voert een Opinie.

Aldus mijn lieve Vrienden, verwachte ick morghen noch eenmael voor haer ghehaelt te worden. Dus bidde ick u dat ghy den Heere voor my bidden wilt, dat hy mijnen mont wil regieren, tot zijnen prijs ende eere. Hier mede wil ick u eewich inde handen Gods bevelen, ende bidde vriendelijck, dat ghy mijn simpele schrijven ten besten wilt houden, want ick en soecke niet dan uut mijns herten eenvuldicheyt, Godt te behagen, want ick en wensche niet, dan, och mocht ick den Coninck der Coningen, ende den Heere alder Heeren [1.Tim. 6.b.15., Apo.17.b.14., 19.b.16.] dus in mijn beroepinghe behaghen,

*Yet another note from this Mother to her children:*

My children, I greet you very heartily, and return your writings to you, so that you might fulfil your Promise that you made to me in them. Always be obedient to those who instruct you to righteousness and punish your transgressions. Farewell; and with this I bid you "Adieu" in this World, my dear children; fear God and shun all evil.

*Yet another letter to the Friends:*

Oh, my heartily and very dearly beloved Brothers and Sisters in the Lord, I greet you once again with the peace of the Lord, may it remain with you until eternity, Amen.

I am letting you know that these my enemies still always torment me about Baptism, but that they say nothing to me about the Incarnation of Christ. The Dean told them about what I believed, and they asked me nothing except whether I also believed that Christ was the Son of David. I said [Mt 16:16] that he was the Son of the living God. "Ach, ach," said the Dean. The Magistrates asked: "Is it not written: 'from the seed of David according to the flesh' [Acts 13:23]?" The Dean answered them, for I didn't pay attention to them. He often called me a liar, for I resisted him because he could not prove to me that the Apostles had baptized children. They all attacked me together, and said that no one could enter the Kingdom of Heaven unless he had been born of water and the Spirit [Jn 3:5]. They asked me hastily whether I didn't confess that, too. I said: "Scripture was not intended for children, but for adults, who have ears to hear." Then they stood up and said: "You hold misguided Opinions."

So, my dear friends, I expect that tomorrow I will be brought before them once more. I ask you that you will pray to the Lord for me, asking that he will guide my mouth to his praise and honor. With this I want to commend you forever into the hands of God, and I ask kindly that you will regard my simple writings charitably, for I seek nothing but out of the uprightness of my heart to please God. For I wish for nothing but - ach! if I could please the King of Kings and the Lord of Lords [1 Tim 6:15, Rev 17:14, 19:16] in my calling thus,

so waer ick wel ter saligher tijt gheboren. Hier mede vrede, afscheydinghe, na desen tijt niet meer. Houdt dit tot een eewich Adieu.

Hier na is Mayken Boosers te Doornick tot pulver verbrant, ende heeft haer Siele begheven inde handen des HEEREN.

*Een Liedeken van Mayken Boosers*
Nae de wijse: Het daghet in den Oosten.

1  Die op den Heer betrouwen  Psal.25.a.3., Esa.49.c.23,
   Eccl.2.b.12., Rom.9.d.33.
   En quamen noyt ter schandt
   Tsy jonck of out, mannen of vrouwen
   Godt sterckse metter handt.

2  Daer was een vrou hiet Mayken
   Boosers, die wert ghevaen
   Sy heeft getreden denge payken  4.Esd.7.a.7., Mat.7.b.13.
   Ter rechter stadt waert aen.

I would consider myself born at a blessed time. With this I wish you peace, goodbye, after this time no longer. Keep this as an eternal Adieu.

After this Mayken Boosers was burned to ashes at Doornik, and gave her Soul into the hands of the Lord.

## *A Song of Mayken Boosers*
To the Tune: "The Day is Dawning in the East"

| | | |
|---|---|---|
| 1 | Those who trust upon the Lord | Ps 25:3, Is 49:23, Sir 2:10, Rom 9:33 |
| | Were never put to shame; | |
| | Be they young or old, women, men: | |
| | With his hand God strengthens them. | |
| 2 | There was a woman named Mayken | |
| | Boosers: she was captured; | |
| | She trod upon that narrow path, | 2 Esd 7:7, Mt 7:13 |
| | Towards that Godly city. | |

3   Tot haer so is gecomen
    Der Kercken Prochelpaep
    En heeft naet geloove vernomen
    Van dat eenvoudich Schaep.

4   Want sy was niet verschenen
    In zijne Kerck in lang
    Dus maecte hy hem op de benen
    En nam tot haer den gang.

5   (Die vrou had haer gehouden
    Stillekens in haer huys
    Het welc haer niet en berouden
    Al quam daer door het cruys.)

6   Waer is u Kerck (wast seggen)         Vrag.
    Bekent is sy u niet                    Antw.
    Want wist ghijt, sout daer op toeleggen
    Dat ghyse in vree niet liet.

7   Wilt ghy oock wel geloven
    Heeft hy gesproocken fijn
    Dat alle Heyligen hier boven
    Int Hemelrijcke zijn.

8   Sy had sulcx niet gelesen
    Gaf sy te verstaen soet
    Maer gelesen had sy van desen
    Int boeck der wijsheyt goet.

9   Der gerechtiger sielen         Deut.33.a.3., Sap.3.a.1.
    Sijn in des Heeren hant
    Sdoots pijn sal haer niet om vernielen
    Roeren aen eenich cant.

10  Veel quamen haer bevechten
    Met menigherley list
    Weerlijck en geestelijcke knechten
    Loos Vossen Antichrist.

3   And so to her there came
    The Church's Parish Papist,
    And he inquired about the faith
    Of that Sheep so simple.

4   For she had not made an appearance
    In his Church for quite some time;
    And so he stirred those legs of his
    And made to her his way.

5   (The woman had herself been keeping
    So quietly in her house,
    And this would cause her no regret,
    Though the cross were her reward.)

6   "Where is your Church?" (was what was said);   Qu.
    "Not known to you, is she;                      An.
    For if you knew, you'd do your all
    To see that she would have no peace."

7   "Do you also believe, indeed,"
    He spoke so nice and fine,
    "That all the Saints, here up above
    Are in the Heavenly Kingdom?"

8   She hadn't read that sort of thing,
    She let them know, so sweetly;
    But she had read the following
    In wisdom's book so good:

9   "The souls of all the righteous,          Dt 33:3, Wis 3:1
    Are in the Lord's own hands;
    The pains of death, for their destruction,
    Shall not touch them from any side."

10  Great numbers came to oppose her,
    With many a crafty trick;
    The servants of both world and church:
    False Foxes of the Antichrist!

| 11 | Maer sy stont haer vianden
Tegen, als een Heldin
So dat sy al quamen ter schanden
Die tot haer wilden in. | Psa.31.b.19. |

| 12 | Monsiuer Massaert, met Schepen
En noch een weerlijck man
Hebben de saeck ooc aengegrepen
En streden Mayken an. | |

| 13 | Dat sy waer van die quaetste
Sect, die ter werelt was oyt
Maer sy swichten voor haer int laetste
Door Godes woort gedoyt. | Act.24.a.5. |

| 14 | Het is claerlijck gebleecken
Dat sy schreyden een paer
Ja dat sy nau meer conden spreecken
Sijnde verwonnen gaer. | Act.6.b.10. |

| 15 | Dus zijnse int laetst ghescheyden
En ginghen vrientlijck heen
Want daer langer niet te verbeyden
Was, dan oneer alleen. | |

| 16 | Broeders looft, prijst Gods wercken | Psa.103.a.2., Tob.12.c.20. |

Sonder ophouden seer
Die dus wonderlijck coemt verstercken
Sijne Ledekens teer.

FINIS.

| | | |
|---|---|---|
| 11 | But all of these, her enemies, She did withstand, that heroine, So that all those were put to shame Who wanted to persuade her. | Ps 31:17 |
| 12 | Monsieur Massaert, with his Sheriffs And another with worldly power Took on this case as well, Attacking Mayken scathingly: | |
| 13 | That she was of the very worst Of sects ere in this world existing; But in the end to her they yielded, Their hardness melted by God's word. | Acts 24:5 |
| 14 | It was clearly evident, That one and all they cried, Yes, they could barely speak a word, So fully were they overcome. | Acts 6:10 |
| 15 | Thus, at the end, that's how they parted, Went away most amiably, For all that could have lingered longer, Was dishonor alone. | |
| 16 | Brothers, bless and praise the works of God, Greatly, without ceasing, Who comes so wondrously to strengthen His little Limbs so frail. | Ps 103:2, Tob 12:20 |

# MAEYKEN WENS

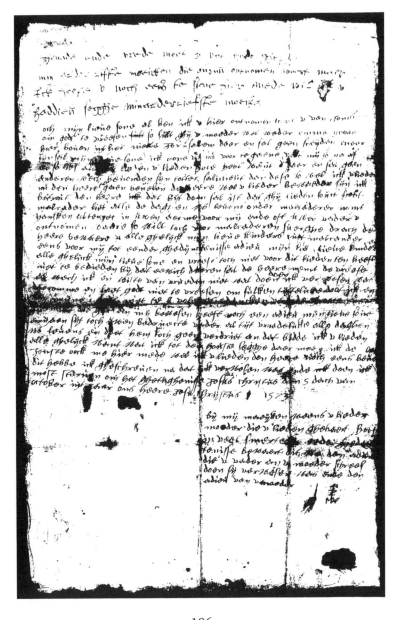

# MAEYKEN WENS[1]
(burned in Antwerp October 6, 1573)

[1] The page on which is found the note to Maeyken, and her letter to her son, has been reproduced also as illustration. These two notes are transcribed with as little intervention as possible: we have not adapted to modern convention the u/v/w and i/j letters, or capitalization and punctuation; the words stricken out have been shown as such; letters or words included above the line have been transcribed in superscript. Through this, readers can get some flavour of how the original might have read, and use the illustration as the basis for trying a hand at transcription themselves. The duress under which Maeyken's letter was written seems evident in details like words which have been crossed out (e.g. lines 2, 8) and inadvertent repetition (e.g. "sal" in line 3 repeated in line 4). Because the fragile paper has been folded many times, letters on the folds are sometimes undecipherable (indicated by including likely letters as []) or decipherable only in the original, and we express heartfelt thanks to Willem Kuiper for checking our transcription against it. Maeyken's signature at the end of the letter has not been reproduced.

*Note to Maeyken from a niece or nephew*

ghenade ende vrede moet v van godt gheschen min alder lifste moeiken die ons nu ontnomen woert maer ick hoepe v noch eens te siene hier mede wil ick v haddieu segghe min alderliefste moeiken

*[Letter to her son Adriaen]*

och mijn lieue sone al ben ick v hier ontnomen scuct v van joncs om godt te vreesen ~~sult~~ so sult ghij v moeder wel weder omme hebbe hier bouen int het nieue jerusalem daer en sal geen sceijden meer sijn sal mijn lieue sone ick hope v nu voor te gaene volt mij so na ~~af~~
5  al so lief al[s] [g]ij lieden u lieden siele hebt want ~~d~~ daer en sal geen anderen wech beuonden sijn totter salicheijt dan dese so wel ick ulieden nu den heere <sup>te</sup> gaen beuelen de heere wel u lieder bewaeder sijn ick betrout den heere ~~ick~~ dat hijt doen sal ist dat ghij lieden souct hebt malcader lief alle de daghen ws leuens onder malcaderen nemt
10  hansken altemet in uwen aerme voor mij ende oft uwen vader v ontnomen waere so wilt toch voor malcaderen suerghe drach de heere bewaere v alle ghelijck mijn lieue kinders cust malcander eens voor mij tot eender ghedijnckenisse adieu mijn lie lieue kinder<sup>en</sup> alle ghelijck mijn lieue sone en vreest toch niet voor dit lieden ten heeft
15  niet te bedieden Bij dat eewich dueren sal de heere nemt de vreeste al wech ick en wiste van vrueden niet wat doen <sup>doen</sup> ick verwesen was daeromme en laet godt niet te vreesen om sulken tijttelicke doot ick en can mijne[n] godt niet te ~~l~~ vole ghedancken van de groete ~~ghena~~ ghenade die godt an mij bewesen heeft noch een adieu mijn lieue sone
20  arijaen sijt toch uwen bedruecte vader al tijt vriedelicke alle daghen ws leuens en doet hem toch geen verdriet an dat bidde ick v lieden alle ghelijck want wat ick tot den houste segghe daer meen ick de jonste oock me hier mede wel ick u lieden den heere noch eens beue<sup>len</sup> dit hebbe ick gheschreuen na dat ick verwesen was ende ~~ick~~ doen ick
25  most steruen om het ghetughenisse jesus christus den 5 dach van october int jaer ons heere jesu chrijstus 1573

*Note to Maeyken from a niece or nephew:*

Grace and peace must be to you from God, my very dearest auntie, who is now being taken from us. But I hope to see you again. With this I want to bid you farewell, my very dearest auntie.

*Letter to her son Adriaen:*

Oh, my dear son! Although I have been taken from you here, if you will turn yourself to the fear of God from your youth, you will have your mother again in the new Jerusalem up above; there there will be no more parting. My dear son, I hope now to be going before you, [follow me in this if you, all of you, love your souls], for there is no other path to salvation than this one. And now I want to commend all of you to the Lord. The Lord will be the keeper of you all; I entrust this to the Lord, that he will do this, if you will indeed seek him. Love one another all the days of the lives that you are with one another. Do sometimes take Hansken in your arms for me; and if your father should be taken from you, take care of one another. The Lord keep you all of you, my dear children; kiss one another for me as a remembrance of me. Farewell, my dear children, all of you. My dear son, there is no need to fear this suffering, for compared to that which remains eternal it signifies nothing. The Lord takes away all fear; I was almost beside myself with joy when I was sentenced. Therefore never cease fearing God on account of this timely death; I cannot thank my God [sufficiently] for all the [mercies] which God has shown me. Here is yet another goodbye, my dear son Adriaen, be kind to your sorrowing father all the days of your life, and do not cause him any pain. I ask all of you the same thing, for that which I say to the eldest, I mean also for the youngest. With this I want to commend you once again to the Lord.
I wrote this after I was sentenced and when I was about to die for my testimony for Jesus Christ, the 5th day of October in the year of our Lord Jesus Christ, 1573.

```
             bij mij maeijken weens u lieder
             moeder die u lieden ghebaert heeft
             in veel smerte tot eeder ghedach
  30         tenisse bewaert dit wel den adieu
             die u vader an u moeder schreef
             doen sij verwesen was ende den
             adieu van u moeder
```

[*Last farewell from Mattheus Wens to his wife Maeyken*]

Hiermeede wil ick een eeuwighen addieu segghen, oft ick niet meer bi u en quame, dan ick sal mijn best doen. Addieu, myn alderliefte, noch eens oorlof ende addieu, myn alderliefte huisvrouwe, met haeste oft ick noch een male bi u cost comen; ende, ofte niet, soe hope ick u hier namaels te sien. Adieu, myn lief.

By me, Maeyken Wens, your mother, who has borne all of you in much pain, as a token of remembrance. Preserve this faithfully, this farewell, which you father wrote to your mother[2] when she had been sentenced, and the farewell by your mother.

*Last farewell from Mattheus Wens to his wife Maeyken:*

With this I want to bid you an eternal goodbye, if I don't come to you any more, though I will do my best. Goodbye, my very dearest, once more farewell and goodbye, my very dearest wife, with haste if I can come to you yet once more; but if not, then I hope to see you in the hereafter. Goodbye, my love!

---

[2] The reverse of the paper contains the letter from Maeyken's husband to her; we have included the closing words of his farewell. A transcription of the full letter can be found in S. Cramer, "Het eigenhandig laatst adieu van Maeyken Wens aan haar kind," *Doopsgezinde Bijdragen* 44 (1904), 119-120.

# INDEX OF NAMES

## A

Abraham, child of Claesken Gaeledochter 76-77
Adriaen Jorisdochter, Aechtken 33, 139ff.
Aken, Gielis van 74-75
Andriesdochter, Magdalena 33, 139ff.
Anneken 26
d'Auchy, Jacques 30

## B

Baerts, Martha 4, 6, 7, 19, 24, 34, 158ff.
Balten 154-55, 157
Beckom, Mary van 3, 6, 13, 20, 26, 31, 122ff.
Beckom, Jan van 32, 124-25, 134-35
Betken, daughter of Soutken van de Houte 4, 164ff.
Betken, sister of Martha Baerts 158-59
Beverts, Hendrik 95
Boosere, Alaert de 35
Boosere, Hanskin de 35
Boosers, Mayken 4, 6, 19-20, 24, 35, 170ff.

## C

Cat, Barbele de 34
Cat, Mayken de 33-34, 139ff.
Cat, Medarde de 34
Catte, Joos de 34
Claes, Weynken 3, 6, 13, 15, 18-19, 27-29, 40ff.
Claeys, Lijnken 34
Coppin, Nicolaas 45

Corte, Maeyken de 4, 6, 19, 33, 139ff.

## D

David, son of Soutken van de Houte 4, 164ff.
Delden, Ursel van, *see* Werdum, Ursel van
Dircks, Lijksken 3, 6, 13, 16-17, 26, 30-31, 94ff.
Dircxdochter, Lysbet, *see also* Leeuwarden, Elisabeth van 112-13
Dirks, Lijsbet, *see* Leeuwarden, Elisabeth van
Douwe, child of Claesken Gaeledochter 76-77

## E

Eggertings, Willem 33
Emden, Meynaert van 13
Euwessz, Hendrick 30

## G

Gaeledochter, Claesken 3, 6, 16, 30, 74ff.
Gerrits, Soetjen 20
Gerrits, Vrou 20
Gheemont, Assverus van 95
Gielis 26
Goude, Pieter van der 45
Goyvaert 26
Grouwell (Gruwel), Bernard 126-27

## H

Halle, Margriet van 33, 139ff.
Hoffman, Melchior 11, 14
Holland, Governor of 28, 41
Hoochstraten, Count van 40-41
Houte, Soetken van den 4, 7, 19, 34, 37, 158-59, 164ff.
Huysmaker, Lauwerens 156-57

## I

Isaiah, son of Anna Jansz (Esaja = Dutch Isaiah) 3, 6, 29, 64-65, 68-69

## J

Jansz, Anna (Anneken) 3, 6, 13, 15, 19, 21, 25-26, 29, 38, 56ff.
Joris, David 11, 13, 21, 29
Jorisdochter: *see* Adriaen Jorisdochter, Aechtken

## L

Leeuwarden, Claesken van, *see* Gaeledochter, Claesken 16
Leeuwarden, Elisabeth van 3, 6, 15-16, 23, 31, 112ff.
Leiden, Jan van 11
Louvain, Dean of 27, 45
Luther, Martin 10, 21, 24

## M

Mariken 26
Massaert 184-85
Matthijs, Jan 11

## N

Naeltwijck, Dean of 27, 44-45

## P

Pesemaker, Lauwerens 156-57
Pieters, Lijnken 34

## R

Raesveld (Raesvelt), Goesen (Gosen) van 32, 124-25

## S

Segersz, Jeronimus 3, 6, 16, 30, 94ff.
Sicke, child of Claesken Gaeledochter 76-77
Simons, Menno 11, 13-14, 31, 75
Sprincen, Maeyken 33, 139ff.

## T

Tanneken, daughter of Soutken van de Houte 4, 164ff.
Titelmans, Pieter 34

## W

Wendelmoet Claesdaughter, *see* Claes, Weynken 27, 45, 49, 55
Wens, Adriaen 4, 14, 36, 188-89
Wens, Hansken 188-89
Wens, Maeyken 4, 7, 13-14, 17, 19-20, 36, 186ff.
Wens, Mattheus 4, 17, 190-91
Werdum, Hero 32
Werdum, Hicko 32
Werdum, Ursel van 3, 6, 20, 26, 31-32, 122ff.

# INDEX OF PLACES

## A

Alberta, Canada 25
Amsterdam 6, 7, 11, 13, 36, 75
Antwerp 3-4, 6-7, 9, 13, 19, 26, 32-34, 36, 75, 95-97, 101, 138-41, 143, 145-47, 187
Austria 10, 14

## B

Basel 11
Bruges 164-65
Brussels 24
Burgundian Court 129

## D

Delden 3, 123-25, 128-31, 134-35
Deventer 125-27
Doornik 4, 35, 171

## E

East Frisia 31-32, 127
Emden 11
England 19, 45

## F

Friesland 6, 31, 37, 75, 112-13

## G

Germany 10-11, 14-15, 18, 25, 27, 29-30, 32, 38
Ghent 4, 33, 35, 150-51, 159, 165
Groningen 11

## H

Haarlem 11
Habsburg Empire 9
Hague, The 3, 6-7, 27, 40-41, 50-51
Hoboken 144-45

## I

Ijsselmeer 75
Ijsselmonde 26

## L

Leer 31
Leeuwarden 3, 6, 11, 31, 75, 88-93, 112-15
Lier 26
Louvain 27

## M

Maastricht 33
Medemblik 20
Monnickendam 28, 40-41
Münster 10-11, 13, 15, 29

## O

Oudenaarde 34, 37, 161, 164-65
Overijssel 125, 127

## R

Rotterdam 3, 13, 20, 26, 29, 38, 57, 64-65, 68-69, 75

## S

Strasbourg 11, 14
Switzerland 10, 14, 45

## T

Tienge 31

## U

Utrecht 22, 123, 124-25

## W

Wervik 33-34
Woerden 40, 41
Workum 75

## Z

Zierikzee 33
Zuider Zee 75
Zwolle 127

# INDEX OF SUBJECTS

## A

advice writing, *see also* testament 19
antichrist 34, 108-109, 183
Augustinians 35

## B

Babylon 34, 59
ban 11
Baptism 9-13, 34, 75, 77, 79, 81, 85, 87, 91, 113, 117, 129, 171, 173, 179
   adult 9-12
   infant, child 12, 34, 75, 77, 79, 85, 87, 117, 173, 179

## C

Calvinists 9, 13, 22-23
Carmelites 35
Catholic Church 9, 12, 16, 23-24, 30, 34, 75, 77, 79, 113, 171, 183
children 4, 12, 17-19, 29-30, 33-36, 59, 61, 63, 69, 75, 77, 79, 81, 85, 87, 97, 99, 111, 133, 143, 153, 165, 167, 169, 173, 175, 177, 179, 189
Christ, humanity of 12, 173, 175, 179
confession 12,

## D

deaconess 31
Devil 41, 53, 77, 79, 83, 133

Dominicans 35, 43, 127, 135

## F

fasting 12
Franciscans 35

## H

host 10-11, 81, 91
Hutterites 25

## I

inquisition 11, 13, 16, 18, 27, 28, 30, 34, 37
   inquisitors 3, 10, 16, 27-28, 30-34, 45, 77, 79, 81, 89, 91, 137, 171

## L

Last Days 11, 13
Latin 31, 45

## M

marriage 12, 30, 32, 97, 99, 115
Mary, virgin 12, 34, 173, 175
Mass 12, 45, 107, 117, 129
Melchiorites 11
monks 45, 47, 49, 53, 55, 155
Münsterites 13, 29

## N

New Jerusalem 11, 67, 189

New Testament 31, 81
  Old and New 22, 24
Nicodemism 13

## O

oath 12, 34, 115, 117

## P

pharisee 13
pope, papacy 12, 27-28, 34, 107, 127, 129, 131, 175
pregnancies 17, 30, 36
priest 12, 45, 107, 109, 117, 131, 171, 183
prophecies, prophet 11, 14,
purgatory 12, 34, 175

## R

relic 36

## S

sacraments 12-13, 29, 41, 53, 79, 81, 85, 91, 93 113, 117, 129, 175
Sacramentarian 10, 13, 29
saints 12, 34, 41, 175, 183
Scripture 10, 12, 16, 20, 22, 67, 77, 79, 81, 83, 87, 91, 101, 109, 117, 127, 129, 155, 179
singing 21-22, 24-27, 89, 91, 131
songs 1, 3-6, 19-27, 29, 32-35, 39, 51, 57, 63, 65, 69, 89, 105, 115, 123, 139, 141, 159, 163, 167, 171, 181
Supper, Lord's  91, 93, 117, 131

## T

testament 3-4, 6-7, 29, 65, 69, 165-67, 175,
  *see also* advice writing
torture 16-17, 25, 31, 33, 36, 95, 107, 117, 119, 149, 151, 157, 171